The Journey

Stan's Story from Death to Perfection

BILL RUEGER
LOUISE TRAVIS

One person's focus to achieve what some would say is impossible
A mother's everlasting love, hope, and faith
Love and support of family
A community of people contributing and serving
Anything is possible!

Everyone, everywhere—listen up! Here's a story of hope. There's no silver spoon in hand. You gotta want it, know that you can achieve it, and act as if you are achieving it, even when you think you can't. Have faith!

In the 1960s and 1970s, Stan was growing up with his brothers in an average American home in an average American neighborhood twenty-five miles north of Philadelphia, Pennsylvania. In February 1986, life for those in this home changed drastically. Stan was in a car crash. His friend, the driver of the pickup truck he was riding in, lost control and the truck rolled eight times. Stan was ejected and was critically injured. He had a long list of obstacles facing him: seven surgeries, three of which were on his brain. During one surgery the doctors took out part of his brain. He died twice. Two of the surgeries were on his leg. He shattered his femur and had a twelve-inch stainless steel plate put in that had thirteen screws and bolts. He completely lost his entire right side, including his speech, and had to relearn everything. He was in a coma for eight weeks and in the trauma/intensive care unit for three months at Abington Memorial Hospital (AMH) in suburban Philadelphia. He had pneumonia three times, as well as bruised lungs, one broken shoulder, and multiple facial bone fractures. He contracted chronic hepatitis after requiring eighteen units of blood. He spent five and a half months at Bryn Mawr Rehabilitation Hospital (recognized as the best brain injury rehab program in the nation) in Malvern, Pennsylvania.

Today, he has a seizure disorder, stumbles, is blind in his left eye, and has one-quarter vision in his right eye. He takes twenty-four pills a day, which require an hour to organize and consume.

Since his crash, from his trust and faith in his God, by his positive attitude and determination, and due to the love and support of his family, friends, and community, he is very much alive.

The statistics show that the average brain injury person begins to have peak performance in his/her recovery around year fifteen. Stan has continued to progress in what is now his twenty-sixth year.

In this book, you'll follow Stan step-by-step, through his successes and failures, on his journey back to life. In it are contributions from family, friends, and the medical and religious communities. They talk about their professions, working with and knowing Stan, and their belief in what most people call the higher power that is present in the world — God. Also provided are real strategies that brain injury patients and their families might use to assist their loved one in his/her quest to return to everyday independent living. Finally, Bill comments about the spirit in each of us. The spirit that is who we are, and without *It* we wouldn't exist. And, what growth and change man can create when man taps this power.

Welcome to a story of love, faith, and hope, and the journey of connecting the dots, one day at a time, back to life. From learning to peel an orange, to learning to speak and walk again, to water-skiing and bowling thirteen consecutive strikes for a perfect 300 game...

The Journey

Twice Dead in 1986
Stan Travis Bowls 300 in 2011

Stan's Story from
Death to Perfection

3/17/13

Dear Sister Ann Patrice
    I'll never forget your faithful prayers during + since Stan's accident I'd see you at morning mass + give you the prayer need for that time + situation. You'd take it back to the other sisters + they'd pray for it too. You're all part of our miracles. We'll never forget you + will always be greatful the Lord put you in our lives

God bless + guide you always
Love + Prayers
Doc & Louise Travis
+
STAN TRAVIS!!

Contributors

Louise Travis, Stan's mother
Dr. Stan Travis, Stan's father
Helen Kannengieszer, Louise's sister and Stan's godmother
Dr. David Travis, cardiologist and Stan's brother
Dr. Thomas Armstrong, ophthalmologist
Sue Ann Butts, teacher, family friend, and neighbor
Theresa Scholly, Louise's cousin
Linda Cahill, family friend
Andy Dooley, neighbor, family friend, and brain injury survivor
William Little, general manager of Thunderbird Bowling Lanes
Mark Cola, certified brain injury specialist
Dr. Anne Saris, gastroenterologist
Dr. Paul Sweterlitsch, retired orthopedic surgeon
Dr. David Long, behavioral neurologist, brain injury medical director
Dr. David Pagnanelli, neurosurgeon

Table of Contents

ACKNOWLEDGEMENTS

This book is dedicated to others who are walking a similar journey. May they always be encouraged and inspired to never give up and to keep the faith.

We'd like to thank our family and friends for all their help, support, and prayers. Thank you to all the doctors, nurses, support staff, and therapists without whom we would not be where we are today. Prayers went up from all over the world, even missionaries in Papua New Guinea. I've seen people with a lot fewer injuries than Stan who are much worse off than him in terms of recovery. Oh, the power of prayer! I often kid that one day, when I'm with my Lord, I'm going to say, "Have you got a minute? Can we talk? There's a lot I didn't understand down there."

There are as many inspirational stories out there as there are survivors. This is just one of them.

The Journey to Perfection
From Death Back to Life
(Through the Eyes of Loved Ones)

We'd also like to thank those who were kind enough to e-mail material to Bill Rueger in France. These helpers are: Sue Ann Butts, Kelly McGowan, Kim Day, Mike Day, and Anne Day. A very special thanks to my sister, Helen Kannengieszer. Her journal was such a valuable piece of information. She kept it for her own mental health during it all. It seems the Lord had her do it for this very purpose, unknown to us at the time. Thank you as well to her son and the "geek squad."

All these people overcame the obstacle of getting material to Bill from Louise in Pennsylvania, who did not have a computer or e-mail. Bill's great phone plan, the postal service, and air travel all made this book possible as well. It just goes to show that when the Lord wants something done, any and all challenges can be overcome. All things are possible with him. Me writing is laughable, I who was only average at best in school in English. And, we are talking about a woman who can't stay awake long enough to read at night. The Lord does have a sense of humor.

Louise Travis

Bringing together such a dynamic group of people with different busy schedules, living around the globe, can be no easy task. However, it worked. We live in a world today with so many incredible tools at our disposal to pull off an undertaking such as presenting to the world this wonderful story of focus, hope, and love. It has truly been an awesome experience to interact with everyone involved. The end result was always very clear in my mind. I had no idea how I was going to manage it, but it happened. We put one foot in front of the other, always moving forward.

This story has a special place in my heart because I grew up in the same neighborhood as Stan, lived a similar personal, social, family, and athletic life as he did, and grew up with Doc as our family doctor.

My wife, daughter, stepchildren, brothers, sisters, stepmom, and father were all very important to me during the writing of this book, and my extended family as well. You are all a very big part of who I am. I love you all.

As with the first book of short stories, the French countryside, the farmers and neighbors, and even more, the French people and colleagues at the different companies where I have been coaching English have always provided the push I needed to drive forward with this project. Some of you have become friends in the process. One has become a special friend. This process of being on a path, making decisions, and accepting all the goodness, joy, and love that come to me is an awesome experience—a spice of life. It makes me smile and laugh. I love it.

Louise and I are connected. On August 1, 2012, she woke to the rock group Journey playing on the radio. The song? "Don't Stop Believin'." This song, which has been on a mix of hers, was a reminder for her. The interesting thing is that this song was on a mix I have been listening to at our French farm and during the drive into Toulouse since January 2012.

And so it goes with everything in life, what we think about comes about. I'll continue to look to nature, silence, animals, and people for inspiration and to see the abundance of love that exists in the world. Life is good.

Bill Rueger

BACK-SCRATCHING

I stood at the huge kitchen window smiling from ear to ear. I was wearing that grin that people who know me, know very, very well. I was feeling happy and connected. I was looking at the family of three ponies in the front paddock one hundred meters from the window.

There were so many other sights and sounds to take in, but I was watching these three ponies with unconditional love. I was observing how content they seemed to just be. They were in the shade of a giant old oak. The air was windless. It was hot. Abnormally hot for early September in the South of France. They had just finished eating, drinking, and grazing. The three were doing a kind of back-scratching, but not the actual act I had observed oh so many times in the past. But, Carlos, Carla, and little Carlito were supporting one another, showing their love in a similar manner. They were whisking the flies from the other's face with their tails.

The four-year-old mama who was pregnant with her third, this papa who was just about the best papa alive (strong and powerful, but knew when to rest), and this little three-month-old were a happy family. They were perfect. They harmoniously existed with all the other farm animals that made their way under the fence into their paddock. They were whole and complete. There was nothing they wanted. They were love, and I was watching it.

I shook my head in amazement. *It* was so cool to watch. They were standing head to tail, north to south, directly side by side. Carla was in the middle facing south, Carlos to her right facing north, and Carlito to her left facing north. The three were swinging their tails back and forth as they usually do. This time, though, they were swishing the flies off the other's face as well as hitting them off the other's back. They were supporting each other, loving each other, and knew they could count on each other — always. This was how they acted — always! *It* was natural and simple. *It* was their instinct to be this way. You could call it a kind of back-scratching.

I was shaking my head with that grin, that stare, that focus, like a pitcher knocking off twenty-seven straight batters, an Ironman triathlete in the zone and on a mission, or a bowler bowling a perfect 300 game. Focus.

As I was thinking gratefully about my years as a triathlete, I was recalling a short story about Stanley (Stan) Travis III, who had bowled a perfect game back in 2011. Stan and I had a lot in common. We were about the same age, grew up in the same neighborhood, and enjoyed sports, cars, and being very active. We both had newspaper routes. Stan was the oldest of three boys while I was the second-oldest of four boys and one girl. Stan's dad was my family doctor. Doc lived thirteen doors down the street. Stan and I had a love for family and enjoyed special relationships with our moms. You could say we had a passion for life. We were the kind of guys that always thought about possibilities; enjoying people, and showing up with a smile even if our asses fell off. We both played organized team sports and pickup neighborhood sports. We both worked at supermarkets. Yeah, we sometimes got in trouble. Sometimes we got ourselves in jams, big jams. Ah yes, remember when we were both in separate car crashes in our youth — me in 1982 and Stan in 1986. Stan was a passenger while I was a driver. Stan's condition was much more critical than mine. And there was more…

I want to share with the world the amazing mind of man and the love and goodness that exists in the world. Stan's story is just one example of many. It is one that is going to be told to represent all those that go untold.

I am going to share with you the life of Stan, his immediate and extended family, his friends and neighbors, and the extensive team of medical-related men and women who have come together to show their passion for serving one another. Stan's story demonstrates perfectly the powerful message of how we as people can create change and growth in our lives. His story powerfully shows the truth about the ideas in the fourteen short stories in my first book:

The Adventures of Fipsila USA – France
One of the short stories is about Stan: "The Perfect Game."

In this book, I am only thinking about how in life there is so much good. Of course, I know there is pain, but with that pain there is growth and change. That growth and change can lead to more good. I want to have a look at the harmony and happiness in life, and the strength and power that people have within themselves. In the midst of pain, I want to take a look around for the wholeness and perfection that there is in the world and within us. We may seem alone at times, but we are all in this together. Love is always here, there, and everywhere. No matter what, keep that childlike love — no matter what. Always remember to scratch each other's back. Love yourself first and then your love will overflow to others, naturally. In times of pain, reach out to your God even more than usual. Whoever or whatever *It* is for you — reach out. This God is everywhere and in everything at the same time. He is life and he is love. I am thrilled to present to you:

The Journey: Stan's Story from Death to Perfection

Bill Rueger

CHAPTER ONE

PERFECTION, BIRTH, AND ADVERSITY

M an and creation. There comes a time in people's lives when they become aware that they did not create themselves. They know, though, that God, this life force, is inside them. He is in every cell, every fiber of their being. When humans really get this fact, then they have entered the world of the spirit. What's more, the more they stay connected in this way, the more powerful they become to create a greater good. Everyone they come in contact with becomes aware of how irresistible they are. In other words, these people are filled with love and it radiates from them.

Bill

On November 7, 1963, Stan arrived, to the delight of his family, weighing in at seven pounds fourteen and a half ounces and twenty-one and a half inches long. His home was with Mom (Louise) and Dad (Stan Sr.) in a second-floor apartment in the

West Oak Lane part of Philadelphia. His dad was a fourth-year student at the Philadelphia College of Osteopathic Medicine. Stan enjoyed sitting in his high chair watching children play in the lot across the street, and moving only an inch or so in his walker because only his big toe on one foot touched the floor.

The day before Dad's graduation and the move to Michigan for his internship, Stan somehow suddenly reached the floor with both feet, put it all together, and took off down the hall. To Mom and Dad's shock, Stan's walker tipped over, and it and Stan fell down a full flight of wooden stairs. Later that night at a graduation party at school, they received a phone call from Louise's sister who was babysitting Stan. He was running a fever and crying a lot. They rushed home and spent the entire night at the hospital. The whole graduation day they fought back tears and tried to keep the accident a secret, not wanting to spoil the celebration for anyone else. All the while, they were calling the hospital regularly to check on him.

Stan had broken his collarbone and had to have his shoulder strapped and braced. Family members helped the three pack up for their move to Michigan, and they took the long route, stuffed in and leaning somewhat forward in the front seat, with Stan and parts of his crib in the backseat.

Six months later, Stan's brother David arrived, weighing in at nine pounds three and a half ounces and twenty-two and a half inches long. Stan was thirteen months old at the time. Weaning Stan off his bottle didn't work then; he'd just go over and take his brother's!

After Stan Sr. spent two and a half years at Garden City Osteopathic Hospital for his internship, staying to work in the ER to make some money and doing some work for other doctors, they returned to Pennsylvania. With help again from family, they moved into their new home in Horsham. (In August 1968, brother Kevin was born. Mom miscarried once before and once after Kevin.)

It was a great neighborhood, with lots of children to play with. Friends and family were close by. Stan was a typical little boy. One time while he was staying with his grandmother, he broke his thumb at the playground and it needed to be put in a cast. A few days later, while Louise was looking out the kitchen window, she saw him climbing up the neighbor's extension ladder with one arm, the other in a cast. The neighbor was standing on the second-floor roof doing some routine maintenance. Stan loved playing organized sports and was at home with the very close-knit group of neighborhood kids. He played baseball, basketball, football, and bowling. During the neighborhood pickup football games, the kids would gang up and tackle him because he was so strong. With the kids still hanging on, Stan would just keep running, dragging them all along with him.

Stan and his family loved boating and water-skiing. Stan was the best water-skier on the lake, making low cuts putting up a wall of water, jumping across the water from one side of the boat to the other, holding the rope handle on his foot, and skiing on one leg with no hands. He skied the entire fifteen-mile-long lake on one ski two and a quarter times nonstop while still making cuts. He often stayed up so long his brothers were tired of waiting for him to fall so they could ski. They asked Mom to cut the engine on the boat and dunk him back into the water so they could get their turn.

As he got a little older he had a newspaper route. In high school, he was on the audio-visual team and the bowling team, and he enjoyed wood shop. He worked at a burger and chicken joint—Gino's. He liked working on cars. Once, Stan, his brother David, and some neighborhood kids took the engine of Mom's car apart and cleaned it up with some oven cleaner.

After graduating high school, he went to school for woodworking, cabinetry, and building in Scranton, Pennsylvania, with a buddy. Friends suggested he take up automotive since he liked working on cars so much. He took a year off to think about what path he would take and worked at a supermarket chain (Acme). Stan then went to Pennco Tech Institute for automotive studies and to do state automobile inspections. By this time, Stan had a social life, including girlfriends, and ultimately he got engaged.

After graduating from Pennco, he got a job at a Cadillac/Oldsmobile dealership in Doylestown, Pennsylvania. They really liked Stan, and soon he was promoted to service advisor. They were grooming him for management. During lunch, he'd work out at a gym and sneak in a quick nap. He was so strong he could do one-armed push-ups off the floor with his feet on the bed like Rocky. (The doctors said that Stan being in such good physical shape at the time was probably the only reason he survived the crash.)

Stan was easy to get along with, pleasant, and well liked (as was demonstrated when he had his accident; people just came out of the woodwork). He was affectionate. He'd come home, find Louise, and lift her up off the floor in a big bear hug and give her a kiss.

Shortly before the crash, Stan was driving his mom crazy trying to straighten out his finances. He'd write a check and not deduct it from the check register. He'd just go by what the bank showed his balance to be when he did his banking. It was a total mess.

Louise would say (after the crash), "I wished he was home to drive me nuts over his finances. Instead, I'd find myself wandering into his empty room...just wanting him home. I used to be able to kiss his boo-boos and make them all better, but it's not working anymore."

Broken hearts are like broken dreams. Each day we can choose to positively anticipate more good things that day which will transport us closer to a dream. Goals, dreams, missions, call them what you like. They give us purpose, something to live for, and when we become passionate about them — slam dunk. Anything is possible. Remember to include God in your plans. No matter what happens in our lives, it may be best to always accept our part in what has happened. With this acceptance can come the about-face that's necessary to spark the fire, the light that is the spirit of our God inside us, driving us to soar to new heights — no matter what has just happened. No matter what.

Bill

A week prior to the car crash on February 27, 1986, Stan was run off the road on his way back from work. A driver had run a red light and Stan went up onto the sidewalk to avoid the crash, nearly hitting a telephone pole. He sustained a neck injury. Louise went to pick him up, as Stan's Corvette couldn't be driven. A witness stayed at the scene, giving the police a report that Stan was not at fault. Stan was put in a cervical collar at the emergency room and saw a doctor for follow-ups, as he was experiencing headaches. A week later, he came home complaining about the headaches and pain. He was to go out clubbing with his friends that night. Louise asked him to stay home because of the pain and the fact that he hadn't felt well all week. Stan didn't take Mom's advice. When his buddy picked him up, Louise told him about Stan's pain. Mom's parting words were, "Please take good care of him for me." He said he would, and off they went.

She went to her regular charismatic prayer meeting, and Dr. Travis (Doc) was not at home. Returning that night, she was tired and decided to change into her bedtime attire, and put on her robe to relax and wait for Stan's return. The entire time she was waiting for him, she was thinking to herself that she shouldn't, but she had the habit of always waiting up for them on the sofa. Her husband came in, and shortly after that the phone rang. It was the worst kind of call for a parent. It was the call that would drastically change the Travises' lives forever. It was the hospital. "Your son's been in an accident." Doc questioned the caller. "Yes, I know, last week. What are you talking about?" The caller said again that Stan had been in an accident and was at Abington Memorial Hospital (AMH). Doc asked the caller if Stan was okay and was told, "Stan had broken his leg. You can come down if you want." Doc told his wife and she immediately went up to dress again. Doc didn't want to wait for Louise, but she insisted. As Louise remembered what she had been thinking and feeling earlier, she grew quite anxious. On the way, Doc needed to stop for gas. Louise became even more impatient, and she was thinking that they were not getting there fast enough.

When Doc and Louise entered the ER, and Doc identified themselves and said that they had received a call, the trauma team doctor came over and spoke to him. The team took the Travises back to where Stan was. When Doc saw Stan, he said to the doctor, "You didn't tell me he had head trauma." Recall that Doc had spent two and a half years working in that busy emergency room at Garden City Osteopathic Hospital in Michigan. As soon as Doc looked at his son Stan, he knew that this was serious. His eyes were all swollen and black like a bullfrog's. Those that were working on him stepped out of that area. Louise didn't realize at the time that the staff did that to give them some time with their son. Louise thought they were coming right back, and she tried to stay out of the way so they could work on Stan. The staff gave Louise a seat and she spoke to her son from a distance. The nurse asked if she could give Louise Stan's down jacket, which was getting feathers all over the place in spite of being bagged.

It was quite a while before Louise went through the bag. She didn't realize the coat had been cut off him and that it was full of his blood. It went through her.

They couldn't give Stan anything for the pain because the night was spent doing all kinds of tests on him to find out the extent of his injuries.

The hospital has a pastoral care department. Rev. William Evertsberg, a minister from Abington Presbyterian Church, was on that night. He came back and spoke to Doc and Louise. He and Doc went back and forth all night between Stan and Louise, updating or checking on Louise. (The Travises have kept in touch with him over the years; he is now serving in Greenwich, Connecticut.) At one point during that night, Louise asked him if he could get oil (from the hospital kitchen, if need be) and anoint Stan. He asked if she thought Stan was that bad. She explained that the Catholics no longer anoint for death only, but for healing, too. She wanted to call for prayers, but it was the middle of the night. Louise said a prayer that the Lord would rally her prayer partners to intercede for him. Louise's sister was awakened in the middle of the night, but did not know why. (Later, after her sister had heard this part of Louise's story, whenever she awoke during the night she'd start praying, not knowing if an SOS prayer request had been sent out or not.) As soon as Louise could, she began putting out calls. Louise's pastor was first, then the prayer tree from her prayer group, and family and friends also got the SOS prayer calls. Somehow, all the phone numbers came to mind. Numbers she didn't even know by heart came to mind. The hospital operators were so good at putting all the calls through. Family and friends then started to arrive to wait with Doc and Louise.

Stan had shattered his femur. He needed surgery to put all the pieces together again and to try and save his leg. His lungs were bruised and filling with fluid. The surgery would be long, and they were racing against the clock while this fluid was filling his lungs. Throughout this time Louise cried out to the Lord, "Take my hand and hold on tight. Don't let go. Otherwise, I may fall down the drain and not be able to be what you needed me to be." Louise's rosary became her constant companion. If she wasn't praying (she felt the need to be in prayer constantly), it was in her pocket, and she would either pat it or hold it.

A friend, Gloria Timberlake, told her years earlier that the nuns had said that if you fell asleep saying your rosary, your angel would finish it for you. Louise thought this was cute and she remembered it! There were times that the only way she could fall asleep from sheer exhaustion and not panic that she had in fact fallen asleep, was the thought that her angel had continued to pray.

When her pastor, Monsignor Leon Peck — who would become a regular visitor — arrived at the hospital, she led him to Stan. Louise heard him gasp, and she thought that maybe he didn't expect to see what he saw.

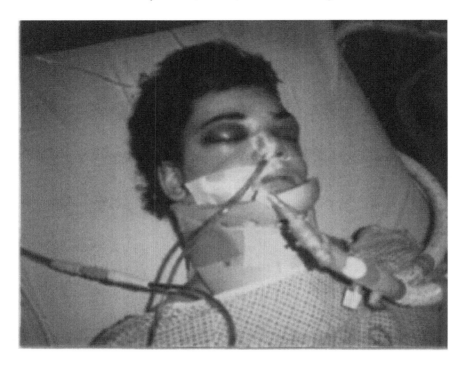

There was a sitting area outside the trauma unit where Louise and the family would wait until they could go see Stan. The doctors would come and talk to Doc Travis, and take him to another area sometimes to talk to him. Louise thought perhaps that was because they could speak about Stan in medical terms, and then Doc Travis could explain things to Louise and the others in layman's terms. Louise also came to see that she would get information on a need-to-know basis. She admitted that, in hindsight, it was best for her, as she could only handle so much at a time. Louise's sister, however, would get very frustrated that they weren't included in these discussions. She'd say, "What do they think we're doing here? Waiting for a bus?"

During those days at the hospital, Louise remembers seeing people she knew and thinking it was a coincidence that she ran into them. One time, for example, she was on her way to eat, and her main focus was simply going to eat and getting back to Stan as quick as possible. It was not until years passed that she realized these people were there to see her, Doc, and Stan. She went on to think, years later, that if she rarely spoke during those times of haste, to please forgive her. She does and did truly appreciate these visits. She also admits to realizing other things as she has reflected on the situation. People would ask how Stan was doing, which she thought was out of courtesy. She recalls probably giving everyone the same one-line answer. If they really wanted to know more, she thought, they would ask more questions. Some didn't inquire at all and she thought they didn't care. She learned later that, in fact, they cared a lot, but they could not stand to see the Travises' pain and maybe didn't want to cry. That worked for her, she thought, since she could not speak about it without crying. However, Doc needed to talk! Louise and Doc would go out and start talking about Stan, and she'd get choked up and fight a losing battle with tears, and would have to walk away.

The Travises would go to Mass at her sister's church, St. John of the Cross, in Roslyn, Pennsylvania, since it was close to the hospital. When they did return to their church, St. Joseph's in Warrington, Pennsylvania, she'd sit in the back and try to duck out as soon as Mass was over, so she wouldn't have to talk with anyone and lose it. She remembers thinking that track runners had a certain number of hurdles to clear, but that someone or something just kept adding more hurdles in front of them—and that it wasn't fair!

The entire staff at AMH was helpful to the Travises, not just the medical personnel. The security people who gave them their car keys, the valet men, the cafeteria staff (the waitress at Friendly's Restaurant), the respiratory staff, lab techs, therapists, pastoral care people, and the cleaning lady were all caring, friendly, and helpful. Ah, the cleaning lady. When they got to the point of trying to stimulate Stan to wake up, she would talk to him as she cleaned the room, even though he was in a coma and nonresponsive. Any of the staff that came into the room did the same. This cleaning lady happened to be just outside Stan's room when he first spoke, and she cried, as did his speech therapist who was writing at a desk outside his room.

Note: Here are some thoughts that Doc and Louise read from literature about patients that were comatose and then became conscious again:

- Some felt trapped and wanted to break out, while others experienced the opposite — they were too tired and peaceful to even care.
- Some had a heightened sense of touch and could feel the negative and positive emotions of the one touching them.
- Some reported that their sense of hearing became sharper.

Here are some suggested guidelines when visiting a patient who is unconscious:

- Assume he/she can hear you.
- Tell the patient who you are and what you are doing there.
- Touch and voice tone can be very meaningful to him/her.
- Put off your visit if you are not in a good mental state.

When the medical team was doing spinal taps on Stan to see if he was any different after the tap, he'd let out a curse word, but they didn't count that, as it was involuntary. The doctor said, however, "Stanley has a nice voice" (even when he cursed at him). A sense of humor is a vital coping mechanism, too, says Louise.

There were times when she would actually think about what would be best at that time. "Do I need a good cry to get it out of my system?" That sort of thing.

Then she thought about 1975, when Doc and Louise took part in a Marriage Encounter Weekend and the Lord touched them powerfully (interestingly, Bill's parents participated in such a weekend the same year, and he remembered how different his parents looked when they came back home). That was followed by Louise taking a Charismatic Life in the Spirit seminar at St.

Catherine of Sienna Church in Horsham, Pennsylvania. Louise came up with a prayer she would say before reading her Bible: "Lord, imbed your word into my memory, mind, and heart that I might feed on it, learn from it, and share it with others in their time of need." During the passing days, weeks, and months at the hospital, she did not realize until later that the Father was doing just that.

Louise admits to not having such a good memory. "I can't tell you what book of the Bible something is in, what chapter or verse. I can only say that somewhere in the Bible it says to give the gift of the message — not an exact quote. I didn't realize the scriptures were being imbedded in me. Yet, when Stan was in the hospital, the Lord would bring to my mind the exact verse I needed to sustain me for the situation. He fed me continually with verses. When I realized what was happening, I started to write them down and put them on the cover of the Mass of Thanksgiving we had for Stan when he came home from the hospital and rehab."

Louise learned after the fact that they never expected him to speak.

One thing about each day is that we are never certain of the outcome or how things are going to turn out. Remember to look at the blessings and not to be so self-absorbed. Hope can come from the fact that we realize we did not create the energy inside us, but rather *It* created us. When we do this, perhaps we do not long for any words, promises, and actions to give us hope. It is the Father, the energy in us, that is our hope. We can trust that the schedule of the master designer is perfect and that we don't need to put our life on hold. We continue to put one foot in front of the other, and what we could not do or have today will appear in the future. Act with faith. Throw away the bad and move ahead with the good.

Bill

CHAPTER TWO

BECOMING WHOLE AGAIN

W e have to be willing. Whenever we begin something new, it takes time, patience, and love to grow and to change toward the goal we have set for ourselves. Every relationship, even with us and God, has a honeymoon period where nothing seems to go wrong. When challenges, obstacles, or difficulties arise, we may want to throw in the towel. It's here that we must dig in and practice patience. It's a matter of laying another layer of the foundation that is going to catapult us to new levels. We never know what is waiting for us around the corner. This is the exciting thing about life.

Bill

Accident – Thursday 2/27 midnight into Friday 2/28
- Broken leg (eight-hour surgery)
- Dislocated clavicle
- Broken first and second ribs
- Skull fracture
- Multiple face fractures
- Lungs bruised

2-28, Friday a.m. Great pain; Stan said it hurts all over. No sedation because of fluid in the lungs. Left for OR at 9:30 a.m. Returned to room at 5:00 p.m. Sedated with respirator.

3-1, Saturday. Reaction to blood – hives.

3-3, Monday. Woke up aware – told Kevin through motions that was his shirt!

3-4, Tuesday a.m. He woke up and pulled everything out: respirator, feeding tubes, IVs, medication, etc. Replaced respirator with oxygen mask. Stan began speaking to us.

Told his girlfriend some guy gave him an oxygen mask. He didn't need it. Said she could have it.

Asked nurse to take off the mask. She responded that she couldn't. He said, "I'll give you my Corvette if you take it off."

Gave his girlfriend a special handshake.

Sat up in chair. Kept patting the bed. Wanted to be a clown.

Helen
Louise's sister and Stan's godmother

3-4, Tuesday. He was a challenge to the nurses. Even if they tied him down, he'd manage to get free and try to remove the tubes, etc. They'd secure him, go out into the hall, and watch him undo it. They laughed at him in amazement and called him Houdini.

Louise

3-5, Wednesday. Speaking more. Concern over fever. Did spinal tap.

Asked girlfriend for a kiss. She kissed forehead. He said, "Kiss my lips." She responded that she couldn't because of the mask. He said, "Kiss my mask!"

Who loves you Stan? "Everybody!"

Tried pulling himself up – asked Norman and Mary for a kiss.

Concern over fever – did spinal tap. Needed to be flat. Woke up and started playing with buttons on bed. Wanted to lie down again.

Helen

The day prior he asked his brother to bring in his Meatloaf (rock-and-roll band) music cassette tape. They had had us bring in his radio/tape player for him.

Louise

8:30 p.m. Ate dinner – soup, pudding. Checking vital signs. Asked to leave. Can come back in fifteen minutes.

Helen

They rushed us back to the family lounge. I knew we needed to pray—hard! I asked for a priest to be called, and dropped to my knees and began leading all of us in the rosary. I don't think I ever said one so fast in all my life. Between being upset and saying it so fast, it's a wonder I didn't hyperventilate. Pastoral care came during all this. I remember her trying to comfort me and telling her I was reciting all the scriptures I could think of, but was having trouble thinking of them all. It was the worst night in all our lives.

Louise

Doctor came out and advised that both pupils were dilated and fixed—not responding. Father (Doc) went flying back and shouted, feeling alarm and fear, trying to get a response from Stan. That is usually a sign of death, according to Doc. They immediately replaced the respirator. He had died, but seemed to come back with respirator.

When he was first told, that Wednesday night, that Stan's pupils were dilated and fixed and that he wasn't responding, Doc jumped up and ran in. We could hear him shouting through the closed door in the waiting room. "STAN. STANLEY. STANLEY.

Wake up! WAKE UP!" He shook him. He rattled the bed. He was totally distraught and inconsolable. He bounced off walls, hit them, banged his head against the wall. He paced while he waited, isolating himself. At one point, he took my hand and I walked down the hall with him, and he said, "What am I going to do? Weesie (Louise) loves him so much. She can't handle this. If he dies it will break her heart. I just don't know what to do. I can't tell her any of this. If he lives, what will we have? It would kill Weesie. Dear God, please spare him. Please, God, let us have him. She doesn't know any of this. I can't tell her."

In many ways, this has been hardest on Doc. He tries to be strong. In the beginning he wouldn't even let Louise near him. He couldn't let anyone hug him. It was as if he had to keep a wall around himself to keep the ocean of feelings from crumbling him. I felt bad because they needed each other, but he couldn't allow it. There were times he just paced alone, and other times in frustration, anger, and rejection of what was happening. He would not allow anyone near him.

Helen

We kept to ourselves a lot, because if someone was able to keep it together, you didn't want to tear him or her down by losing it.

Louise

How it happens is up to him. Faith is king.

Bill

3-6, Thursday, 2:30 a.m. Brain pressure was increasing. Operated. Put ventricular drain in to relieve pressure. This was a night of darkness and pain. Everyone was crying, pacing, sniffing, sobbing, having breakdowns, praying — mouths moving constantly, needing to be alone, not touching, private pain. We had barriers around us and kept to our private space. Like constellations in the sky we kept our distance, but together — together, but separate. We all were experiencing pain, but separately. We were unable to reach out and embrace and console each other after the original shock. But then, upon learning the devastating news, everyone did embrace and cried. Then, we drew apart again to our separate world of prayer. We all prayed constantly. A minister and dear friend of Louise's, Mike Owens, seemed to be able to touch and interact with everyone during that night of waiting.

5:00 a.m. Stan is back in the room. Told to go home and get rest. He will be sleeping with no change.

Helen

5:30 a.m. I had gone upstairs to get ready for bed. My husband had wound the cuckoo clock and was locking up when the hospital called. Stan had died again and was resuscitated. Doc came to the bottom of the stairs and called to me. He said maybe we need to think about someone else now—meaning donating Stan's organs. I jumped up, shook my head, made hand gestures: "NO! NOT NOW!" I ran into our room to dress again and we headed back to the hospital. We called the family again. When we arrived, we met the neurosurgeon, Dr. Pagnanelli, and, doctor to doctor, he and my husband discussed what to do.

I saw Dr. Pagnanelli trying to hide it, wiping a tear away. That tear meant a lot to me. I saw how deeply he cared, and knew he would give Stan all he had and do his very best for him. Stan's dad—my husband, Doc—said to remove the temporal lobe to relieve the pressure and give room for the brain swelling.

That night is indelibly imprinted in my mind. I can still see it all so clearly.

I remember standing there as this was going on. The scripture about God asking Abraham to sacrifice his son to him came to mind. That scripture always bothered me. I couldn't understand how God could ask him to do that—at least, not the Lord that I'd come to know and love and serve.

I said to God in my head, *I'm just not there yet, I don't have that much faith.* That thought was immediately marked in my head with, *Where else can you go?* This was Peter's response to Jesus when he asked if he was going to leave him, too. Inside, I had to give my son to the Lord. There was nowhere else to go but to him. No one else could give me what I needed for my son — only him. I had to trust him and give my son over to him completely.

I can still see Dr. Pagnanelli, getting up and walking down the hallway. He looked so tired after being up with Stan during the first surgery. Now he had to go back to the OR with him and do something he really didn't want to do.

He walked down the hall looking a lot like Rocky dragging himself into the ring for his last couple rounds, drawing on all he possibly could from inside himself.

We had become used to reading the monitors in Stan's room. After that surgery, once he was back in his room and situated, they let us go in and see him. I walked in to see the monitors — flatlined — his tongue hanging out of his mouth, wrapped so it wouldn't dry out. My heart almost stopped. I knew they'd taken out part of his brain. I thought, *Oh my God, what have they done to him?* I didn't realize they hadn't hooked up the monitors yet.

I recall Doc saying to me, "We'll take him any way we can have him, right, Weesie?" Inside, I couldn't agree. I'd often thought how hard it must be on people who'd had a stroke — to be aware yet unable to communicate, like being locked in their body. I couldn't condemn him to that. I told the Lord it was between Stan and him, not me. Later, I'd recall hearing or reading somewhere along the way in my life: "God always gives his very best to those who leave the choice to him."

The cuckoo clock remained wound and stopped until Stan returned home, at which time it was started again — similar to our lives beginning again. Everything in our lives stopped during the time he was in the hospital and the rehab.

Louise

5:30 a.m. Hospital called again. Taking back to OR. The swelling of the brain is increasing. They took brain tissue from the left temporal lobe (controls speech).

Coma partly drug-induced and partly due to swelling. Stan was given drugs every hour to keep brain at rest and in the coma.

Great concern over brain pressure – not stable.

Originally operated on brain when pressure was forty.

Pressure continues to fluctuate. I saw it at two and at twenty-eight. When questioned, the nurse said they wanted it below fifteen. At twenty, they worried.

Stan is reacting to painful stimuli. Respirator breathing tube came out; had to replace. Doctors all perplexed that this happened now. They'll never know the reason without an autopsy.

3-7, Friday a.m. Respirator – tongue began protruding and swelling. Got sneaks to prevent foot drop.

3-8, Saturday a.m. Stopped reacting to painful stimuli. There was such pain and anguish on his father's face. Doc was so upset and worried. We could read that on his face, but he never told us that Stan had stopped responding to painful stimuli. He made the excuse that he was worried about them doing the scan because they would have to lay him down, and when they lay him down his brain pressure goes up. We could see his anguish. When they took Stan down to do the scan Doc went with them. He held on to the bed. When they returned we could see the worry, the pain. We could tell he didn't like the results. He didn't tell us until the next day that Stan had stopped responding to stimuli the day before. He only told us after he began responding again.

He knows so much and tries to spare us—censor the information—and be strong for us all. His heart is broken. Please help him, Lord. Even with all these heavy emotions he keeps his sense of humor. He makes us laugh and gives us a release from tension. God bless him for that, and thank you for this gift, this quality in Doc. Stan's dad goes in and rattles the bed. He yells and shakes him. Kevin, his brother, said, "If I ever get sick and am in the hospital, don't ever tell Dad. Don't let him come to visit. No wonder why Dad wakes him up, he grabs his broken shoulder and shakes him. I would open my eye, too."

Doc goes in now and lifts Stan's eyelid and says, "Hi, Stan!"

Doc blows in his eye.

Doc threatens to dye the long part of his hair, leave the other part shaved, put an earring in his ear, and put him on MTV. Start a new trend, Doc assures us.

Then his dad goes in and arm wrestles with Stan. He made so much noise that the nurses came running to see what the problem was.

Scan showed more swelling in a different part of the brain. The frontal lobe was more swollen than the last time they did the CAT scan. This section was not swollen to this extent the last time the scan was done. Brain swelling increased in the area of the skull fracture. Stan was put on seizure medication and antibiotics.

3-9, Sunday. Removed pressure monitor – not working correctly and a possible source of outside infection.

Started reacting to painful stimuli. One-third of all his blood had been replaced.

Helen

The respirator: whenever they had to move Stan for tests, etc., they'd take him bed and all. He had an entourage of medical staff—two people pushing and directing the bed, people moving his bags (IV), and someone manually squeezing a respirator bag until they got there and could hook him up again. The sight and intensity of it all was frightening.

Louise

CHAPTER THREE

HARMONY AND PUTTING THINGS BACK TOGETHER

When we are in harmony, in the groove, connected, high, we are aware of our surroundings and of what (and who) is in our life to show us a next step, to help us make a decision. Are you bored, ungrateful, unenthusiastic with the world as it is? Wake up! What are you grateful for? Get refocused on doing something that matters for the greater good. Life is rich, full, and abundant. Look to nature, where there is no savings in anything. It is life! It is growth! It is change!

Bill

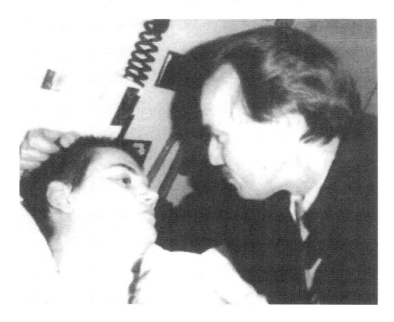

Doc and Stan

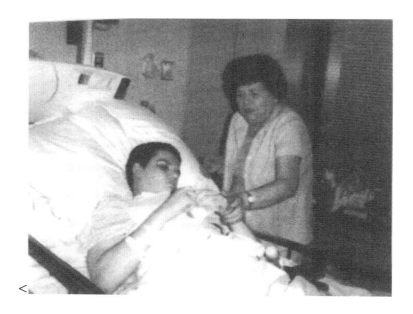

Grandmom Travis and Stan peeling an orange

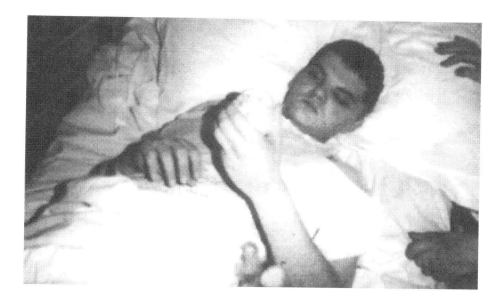

Stan staring at the orange

Stan eating the orange

6-11-86, Wednesday

Speech therapy – reading with 100 percent accuracy. They gave Stan two cards and asked him where he lived. He took the card that read *Horsham*. Every time they asked him a question he selected the card with the correct answer.

Helen

When discharged from Bryn Mawr in November 1986, Stan was reading at a fifth-grade level, with a much lower comprehension due to the need to self-cue each letter in order to get the word. He had to read something at almost every therapy session, but did not read with that frequency as time went on and it got much more difficult.

Louise

6-13-86, Friday

Stan loves the movie *Stripes*. He used to have practically the whole thing memorized. Today he sang a line from the song: "Do wah diddy diddy dum diddy do." What an accomplishment—a real tongue twister.

Helen

When asked by his friends to sing it, I thought, *Yeah! Sure! Impossible!* But he did!

Louise

He was swaying and kind of dancing in his wheelchair with his girlfriend. A line in one of the songs he sang along with was: "Oh, I want you." Also, he was singing to music: "I can't…" Therapy explained that music is a different part of the brain.

6-14-86

Stan Sr. (Doc) kept coaxing Stan Jr. to say, "Hi, Pop!" Finally, he said it—"Hi, Pop!"—much to his dad's delight.

6-15-86

Stan said, "Happy Father's Day!" Family was allowed to go to one of his therapies once per week.

6-18-86

Louise went to therapy again. They had Stan up and using a walker. Since he is unable to use his right arm to support himself on the walker, they rigged the walker up with a flat surface for Stan to rest his arm on. He can hold the edge with his fingers and strap his arm on it from the elbow. Using this, he had hopped about fifteen steps in the morning. When Louise arrived, the therapist asked him if he wanted to show his mom. He did. He hopped a short distance, and the therapist asked him if he was tired and wanted to sit down. Stan shook his head no, and continued staring ahead at some distant goal that he seemed to have in mind. He eventually hopped fifty-five to sixty feet, the entire length of the therapy area.

Helen

Stan didn't actually hop as one might envision. He was not allowed to put any weight on his right leg (shattered femur). His weight was on his arms and left leg. The therapist would walk beside him with her toes under his heel to make sure he wasn't using that right leg which was healing. He would simply touch his right toe on the floor for balance.

Louise

Be silent for ten minutes. Hold an idea, something you are passionate about, in your mind. Concentrate on it. Think only of it. Can you do it? Give it focus. Attention. Do this daily, do what you are passionate about, and let it come to you. Don't think about not having it. Visualize yourself doing it and take the steps toward realizing it. It'll happen. Hold on. Really see the people and things around you. They are there for you. You are drawing them to you. The more in tune we are with the spiritual activity all around us, the more (and the better) we can do our task to reach our goal.

33

What do you want? *What do you want?* WHAT DO YOU WANT? Go get it, now.

Bill

Speech therapy had Stan singing, "Happy Birthday to You." They said it was one of the easiest for Stan to sing. Thinking something and wanting to say it is difficult. He is not always teasing or being uncooperative when he won't say something. It is difficult for him to think of something and then follow through all the processes necessary to say it.

6-21-86, Saturday

Louise and Stan went up the mountains to celebrate their twenty-fourth wedding anniversary. Friday after work David drove up, cut the grass, ran the weed whacker, cleaned and mopped the house, turned their bed down, left two bottles of Asti Spumante on ice, and wrote on a note: "Relax and enjoy – from your three darling sons."

The young people had soda, pizza, and watermelon outdoors at a party with Stan: his brother David and eight friends. Louise said that weekend was the first time they really talked and shared their feelings about this whole thing. Louise said they really couldn't share before this because they each were fearful of bringing the other down. Stan told her that his pulse was racing the night of the brain surgery. His HR was at 155. He could feel his heart pounding in his throat. His medical knowledge made that nightmare all the worse for him. He said if he was ever going to have a heart attack, that was the night.

Helen

6-24-86

A letter showing this date arrived from Abington Memorial Hospital. This letter was in response to a letter Doc had written to AMH about how successful they were in providing outstanding service to Stan and his family. The letter was written by AMH's

34

director of development and public relations, stating what a pleasure it was to serve families as thoughtful as Doc's.

An attitude of gratitude.

Bill

6-25-86, Wednesday – Therapy

The therapists told Louise they will be beginning aquatics
with Stan. Therapy suggested Louise check her insurance to see
if it would cover an overnight pass at home for Stan. If he is covered, they suggested he might be able to go home on the Fourth
of July weekend, since it is three days without therapy and time
will probably hang heavy. Louise called the CAT Fund (a cata-
strophic injury fund) representative. She informed her that he was
covered for unlimited overnight passes. She told Louise to find
out what she would need and get it—a hospital bed, commode,
etc. The representative said that any construction, alterations, or
additions that may be needed for Stan should be thought about
ASAP. They should begin plans and discussions and get prices
from contractors if needed.

Helen

I didn't want to use any insurance money for alterations to
the house that were not absolutely necessary. There was an insurance cap and I didn't want Stan separated from us. Thankfully,
we only needed a second handrail in the house.

Stan had gotten bedsores in the hospital from having to be
somewhat elevated so the pressure in his head wouldn't go up.
I assisted the nurses at the hospital and rehab, learning how to
bathe him in bed, change the sheets with him in bed, assist with
the bedsores, transfer him to and from the wheelchair, dress him,
put on his leg brace—pretty much total care. I even learned how
to reconnect his respirator hose when he'd pop it off in the hospital. All this was a huge help when he came home on his pass.
Even though I hadn't done it, only assisted, at least I knew what
was needed and what to do. I must confess, it was overwhelming doing it until I worked it all out. I told my husband, "I'll do

it all, I just need you to do the bedsores with the sterile technique necessary." Stan was incontinent at the time also.

We ordered the hospital commode, wheelchair and cushion, etc., and set up the living room for him. Bryn Mawr sent all the necessary supplies with us for his bedsores: bed pads, medication, foam blocks that had to be put on his leg/feet when in bed to prevent foot drop. I slept on the sofa and set the alarm every two hours to turn Stan, since he couldn't turn himself. This also prevented more bedsores and helped the ones he had.

I remember the dryer broke during this time and I had to run clotheslines all over to dry multiple sets of sheets, clothes, etc. When all was set up for his visit, I looked in the living room with mixed emotions. I was happy he was coming home, finally, for a visit, but was in disbelief that we needed all this equipment.

I am grateful they let me help and taught me so much. I don't know what I would have done otherwise. I was still overwhelmed as it was.

Louise

To what lengths are we willing to go to accomplish the mission at hand? If we think we can, than we will; and if we think we can't, then we won't. It's pretty simple. Get started now and grow new brain cells. Get 'r done!

Bill

Therapy said she saw Stan move his right ankle for the first time. She was concerned that it would atrophy. Louise kept reminding Stan to eat. He leaned close to her and said, "Knock it off!" Louise explained that therapy shows him words that begin with the same letter; for example, M words like *me, moon, map*. They leave out a letter and Stan fills in the missing letter and says the word.

Psychologists noted that Stan is more depressed – mildly to moderately.

6-26-86, Thursday

Three of Stan's friends from Acme visited. Stan was moved to a new building (Tuesday, June 24). He was eating in the new lounge while we all visited. A new patient in an agitated state was also being fed in the lounge. The new woman whistled, screeched, screamed, and cursed. One of the girls had a key finder on her key ring which is activated by a whistle. Her beeper kept going off, activated by the patient's screeching, screaming, and whistling. The nurse fed her mashed potatoes that she didn't want. She just opened her mouth and let them fall out. The nurse got her a bib. As the bib was put on her, she began begging for help. She looked all around, wailing, "Help!" The nurse assured her that she was okay and that it was just a bib. She declared that she wanted to feed herself. The nurse put the food on the fork and gave it to her. She put the fork in her mouth and just kept it tightly clasped between her teeth, with the handle sticking straight out. They repeated this with each forkful. Stan glared at her when she cursed. She yelled back at him, "What are you looking at?" Someone sneezed; she stopped cursing and said, "God bless you," then continued cursing. Before this, another person had appeared in a wheelchair. He saw the food cart and began to whine, whimper, and cry. "I want that, I want some, I didn't get any. Where is the waitress? Waitress!" I explained to him that the food trays were being given out and he would get his. He continued to cry, moan, and wail. Another patient kept complaining that it was air force food and kept trying to give it to Louise. It was really like a three-ring circus!

Helen

Go inside, be alone, and experience who you are. Just be. Find a comfortable place and, for ten minutes, be relaxed and be still. Be absolutely still. Let your thoughts wander. Gain control of your physical body. Great athletes do this all the time.

Bill

I would drive out daily before rush-hour traffic. There were times I'd go into Stan's room, and if he was uncooperative or agitated, I'd just go out in the hall, wait a minute or so, and reenter as if I'd just arrived. He'd forget that fast and we'd start fresh.

Because things on the floor could be bizarre, we tried to take Stan elsewhere after eating. When the weather was nice we'd enjoy the beautiful grounds. Nature is soothing. If it was bad outside, we'd just go downstairs to the waiting area and visit with whatever guests he'd get.

I remember the man who complained about the food being "air force food." I remember this man standing at the head of a long table where other patients were eating their dinner and he proceeded to "address the troops." He must have been an officer in the air force. Another woman was evidently a business-woman. She would pick up papers and pass them out to people. She thought another patient was her accountant. Some would wait by the door in hopes of sneaking out as staff or visitors came in and left. There was also a padded room where patients in an aggravated state could work it out without hurting themselves. One man talked like Donald Duck.

Three-ring circus is a mild description. At times you needed to get out of there and go elsewhere for your own sanity.

Louise

In the late eighties and early nineties, I worked in the behavioral health field in Pennsylvania and Arizona. This was after I had returned from Central and South America, was transitioning back into life in North America, and had just made some major life decisions of my own. This was the time when I made the decision to pursue the sport of triathlon (I saw the 1989 Ironman in Hawaii on TV), and pursue an educational role in investments and real estate. I could absolutely relate to the chaos that sometimes exists in the behavioral health field.

Bill

6-26-86 continued

Stan is very tired. His responses were not always appropriate. They are taking him off phenobarbital and introducing Tegretol. As they decrease the phenobarbital they increase the other. He is also getting an anti-arthritic drug for his shoulder. The combination has him very tired. At one point Stan wanted to say something to Louise. He leaned close, looked into her face and tried slowly to say something. He would think and try. Louise watched him intently, trying so hard to understand. He tried repeatedly and became increasingly upset. As a calming gesture, Louise said, "It's okay, you are doing good." He shook his head no, rejecting her comment with frustration. The nurse said they are starting a new regime between 8:00 a.m. and 8:00 p.m. Every two hours they will ask Stan if he has to go to the bathroom. They are trying to establish control and communicate concerning this.

6-27-86, Friday
Stan had an appointment with the orthopedic doctor at Abington. Dr. Sweterlitsch is checking for a leg brace and a shoulder brace. The leg brace was prescribed. Dr. Sweterlitsch was aware of the broken shoulder. Louise and Doc were just unaware of this due to a miscommunication.

6-30-86, Monday
Stan sang, "M-I-C-K-E-Y M-O-U-S-E." Speech is controlled on the left; singing on the right. Louise said Stan had a new nurse. And she didn't know that Stan is supposed to get a nap after afternoon therapy. He unstrapped his table, his seat belt, and had one hand on the bed, preparing to try to get into bed himself.

7-2-86, Wednesday
We practiced transferring Stan from the wheelchair to the car.

7-3-86, Thursday
No aquatics due to bedsore – afraid of possible infection.

7-5-86, Saturday
First visit home. Louise and Stan took Kevin's car and the Saab on Wednesday to see which was easier for Stan to get into. The Saab required Stan's right leg to be bent more and the bend was less getting into Kevin's car. Stan shows pain when that leg is bent.

Helen

As we neared our area, Stan recognized the fencing of the Willow Grove Naval Air Base, which is close to our home. He pointed to it and kept saying, "Home! Home! Home!" I teased him that he reminded me of the movie *ET* (phone home). Stan would say this every time he came home.

Louise

November Homecoming
Left to Right: David, Stan, Kevin

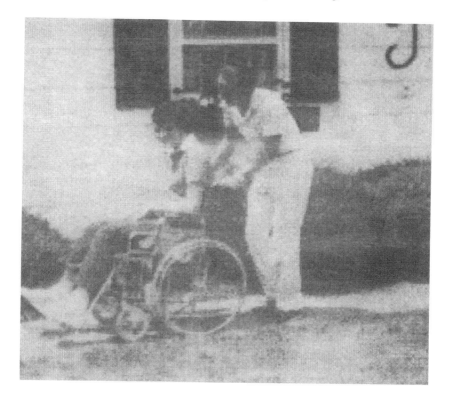

Stan and Doc

He came home and took a long nap. Louise made his favorite dinner, leg of lamb. She said he expressed his enjoyment with every forkful: "Mmm, mmm." The neighbors were outside having a picnic. Doc proudly wheeled him over and surprised everyone. They all gathered and greeted, cheered, and some of us even shed tears. He was pleased to be there.

Helen

Interesting. No coincidence. I am a meat man. One of my favorite farm dishes at Le Blaziet is *l'agneau* — lamb!

Bill

When Louise tried to get him ready for bed he would not allow her to take his trousers off. Doc had to do that. He also didn't want Louise to wash him, although he has allowed her to help with his bedsore. She laid a towel over his lower torso and he allowed his underwear to be removed. He washed himself under the towel.

It is necessary to turn Stan every two hours through the night because of his bedsore. Louise said it is about one and a half inches deep, but in places it is deeper. It has tentacles that spread out and go deeper. It has to be cleaned and repacked three times per day. Doc does most of that. They took turns turning him beginning with Doc at 1:30 a.m., followed by Dave, Kevin, and then Louise.

7-6-86, Sunday

Stan slept until noon. He woke up when they turned him, but when asked if he wanted to get up, he said, "No," and went back to bed. At noon, they got him up and thought he would skip his afternoon nap. He was uncooperative about brushing his teeth, shaving, etc. Everyone tried to get him to do it. He tried to protest or explain, but was unable to communicate. He just kept repeating, "But…no…no…but." He was unable to communicate.

A couple of times Louise had to scold him. He made faces at her, not being able to communicate. Louise told him she understood he was sick, but would not tolerate disrespect. At times, Louise would have to say, "I'm your mother," and Stan would finish by saying, "And don't you forget it!"

Stan became uncomfortable. They adjusted his shorts, his catheter hose, and finally asked if he wanted to go back to bed. He nodded yes. Even in bed he tossed and turned and moaned. They didn't know if it was a result of the folding wheelchair with the lower back, or the lack of the board with the cushions to sit on. They had cushions but no board, and wondered if the canvas sagging hurt his bedsore. The mattress on the hospital bed they rented was not as firm as the one at Bryn Mawr. They thought his back might hurt from that. No one could figure out what was wrong, but his discomfort continued to increase.

On the trip back to Bryn Mawr he moaned and thrashed. They asked him if he could show them where it hurt — touch where it hurt. He touched his leg. When traffic allowed, Doc pulled over and massaged the leg. They thought maybe it was a charley horse. After his return, they found that the Texas catheter had been too tight. His genitals were swollen and covered with ulcers. Louise was concerned that he was unable to communicate where the problem was when asked, after all those hours had passed.

Stan's foot on his bad leg is showing a tendency to turn out. To counteract this tendency they are using a foam boot block that keeps his foot in place while he sleeps. It is necessary to make sure this is positioned correctly when he is turned in his sleep through the night.

At one point he was trying desperately to communicate something to Louise. She couldn't understand, so he tried spelling, "T-M-N-I-..." She still didn't know what he wanted to say, even when she tried rearranging the letters or adding letters. She assured him it was okay.

7-7-86, Monday

Stan was trying to tell Louise something. He stared into her face. She searched his face for the meaning and hung on each sound he uttered. She was desperately trying to understand. He repeated, "I want, I want, I want, I want." She could see him lose the thought. Louise explained that forgetting was part of brain injury and would improve with time. He is still on phenobarbital, Tegretol, and an anti-arthritic. He didn't have a catheter today. They are working with him and the urinal, trying to allow his genitals to heal. He had an "accident" during dinner.

7-8-86, Tuesday

Stan was awake when we arrived. Louise asked him if he wanted to get up, but he declined. When the trays arrived, she asked him if he wanted to get up and eat, and he said, "No." Louise let him go a little longer and then got him up. He seemed too tired to eat. He looked at me with a mixture of disgust and disbelief — kind of like he was thinking, *Do you believe this?* I said,

"No, and here I am," incredulous and at a loss. He seemed too tired to lift the fork or do anything else regarding eating. Louise went to the cafeteria and got him something else, hoping to interest him to eat. Stan's responses were only about 50 percent accurate. He seemed so tired that he didn't understand or was easily confused.

He went to recreational therapy and his girlfriend assisted him in making string art. He seemed more interested in the woodwork project, which was a magazine rack one of the other patients was making. David came and we took Stan outside and played tapes. Stan perked up and kept the beat with his body and played air guitar.

Helen

We used to use music to pump him up and get him moving out of bed. Lionel Richie's "Dancing on the Ceiling" was great for that. He was in concert in the area, so we got a pass and took Stan. They actually had Lionel Richie do a "Dancing on the Ceiling" effect. We were filled with excitement and awaited that, but we had to have Stan back at a certain time. As we were rushing Stan out in his wheelchair we could hear him playing that as the grand finale. We were so sorry we missed that. It was electrifying!

Louise

Is this just another coincidence or a sign of our connection? Stan's a Lionel Richie fan, as am I. The beat rocks! He's all about life being a party, feeling good, and being happy. I have watched Lionel Richie interviews and performances on French national television. The French seem to love him as well.

Bill

A family education head trauma group therapy meeting was gathering that night. I asked Louise if they had ever attended and if they were fearful. She said that she hadn't been—she had forgotten or missed the time and date. I kept my eye on the clock and told her as the time approached. It was announced on the loudspeaker. People came from all directions. I tried to encourage her to attend. I told her his girlfriend and I would visit with Stan, and that David was expected. Stan would be amused. Louise explained that she really was reluctant to give up any time that she had with Stan. I assured her that if that was the problem Stan could attend also, since I've seen many patients in the room. Louise still declined, much to my disappointment. I thought it might be helpful in dealing with Stan's uncooperative episodes, his modesty, and the many problems that were popping up. (When I get the opportunity, I want to mention to Louise that it may be helpful to Stan, since other patients are included and they may verbalize something that he is feeling but unable to communicate. It could be beneficial for Stan even if Louise and Doc don't feel the need.)

Helen

I had learned by that point that it was *best for me* to get information on a need-to-know basis and not to ask questions that I wasn't ready to hear the answers to.

Louise

7-10-86, Thursday

Stan's cousin Steven visited today. He said Stan was still very tired and his responses were not accurate. He agreed that he was also a little bit disappointed that he was still on both medications.

7-12-86, Saturday

Second weekend home. Kevin's graduation party. I was sweeping out the breezeway when Louise pulled up with Stan. She said that as they passed the house, Stan said, "Ah, ah, ah, ah, ah, ah." It was as if the conquering hero was returning. He was sitting tall in the seat, bright-eyed, eager, and filled with anticipation. They put him near the pool where he finished his Burger King Whopper. He was apparently delighted because they stopped at Burger King for lunch. His friend from Pennco Tech visited with him. They put Stan in for a nap, but he seemed too excited to really sleep. Every time someone looked in on him, he opened his eye and peeked to see who it was. As time grew near for the party, he became anxious to get up, and Anne even had to restrain him a few times when he got impatient and tried to get up alone.

He enjoyed the party, the music, and his celebrity status. He accepted every bit of food that was offered to him. He would add it to his tray and keep working his way through it all. He "boogied" to the music and enjoyed wheelchair dancing and playing air guitar. It was nice to have him there and to see him in the middle of all the young people.

Doc had several outbursts and David asked why Dad was so tense. Louise confided that he had been so tense that she feared he may not be well emotionally. She said that he shows this stress constantly and that she is really worried about him.

When I arrived to help today, Louise was still picking up Stan Jr. Doc was there and said, "What do you think of our Stasky? Isn't he doing great?" I hesitated, and then cautioned Doc that I was going to be perfectly honest with him. I confided that I was disappointed and discouraged lately. Stan is more tired, and consequently his responses are not appropriate a greater percentage of the time. I explained that I understand it was probably attributable to the double medication, but that I was still concerned. I also asked why it was taking so long to take him off the phenobarbital if that was indeed their goal. Doc admitted that he really needed to talk with the doctors regarding this. I felt like I was overly negative because everyone that saw him said how great he was doing.

7-13-86, Sunday

Louise and Doc woke Stan about 9:00 a.m. Last week, when they allowed him to sleep until noon, it threw off his medication schedule and bedsore treatments. They were trying to keep him to his schedule this week. It was a better day compared to Sunday the week before. He went back to sleep after the 9:00 a.m. meds and treatment and took an afternoon nap.

He is still very modest with Louise, but will allow Doc and his brothers to help. He will not allow frontal nudity and he wants to keep covered with a towel. His genitals are still sore and he says, "Ouch" when Doc treats it. He contracted epididymitis, which is a swelling (inflammation) of the epididymis, the tube that connects the testicle with the vas deferens. They have to change his clothes and bed since they can't use diapers due to the bedsore.

7-14-86, Monday

Louise also voiced concern regarding Stan's progress. She said he was in Abington three months and Bryn Mawr half of that time, and she is wondering if she should be seeing more improvement or more rapid progress. I have also been concerned, as I mentioned earlier. I have been increasingly concerned that his responses are not appropriate even more often now than in the past. He had reached 80–90 percent accuracy for a while. My last visit he was so tired and the accuracy was only about 50 percent. I hope it is due to the medication and will self-correct once they are changed. I am also worried because on Stan's first visit home, when the catheter was too tight, they spent the entire day trying to figure out what his problem was. In all those hours he was unable to touch, indicate, or communicate in any way what was hurting or bothering him, even though they asked him repeatedly to touch where it hurt to show them. I am really depressed about this. I am also worried because although Stan gets hours and hours of physical therapy every day his bad arm and leg seem to be getting worse. I had hoped for improvement, but he isn't even maintaining; rather, he seems to be deteriorating. Although there is slightly more finger movement, Stan expresses pain when his arm is moved even slightly while it is on his tray, for example. I used to watch the therapists doing range of motion exercises on him in the hospital and he showed no pain, although the motion was on a much greater scale. Now, tiny movements evoke expressions of pain. Also, the foot on his right leg is turning, necessitating the boot be worn while he sleeps.

I am concerned but reluctant to express these fears to Louise and Doc. I am reading the Bryn Mawr book again. It said that patients often continue to improve for several years and that is encouraging. It went on to say that the most rapid improvement usually occurs during the first several months. I was looking for answers, but there doesn't seem to be any. I wish I could talk to the doctors like I could at Abington.

7-16-86, Wednesday
   Physical therapy observation day.
   Stan hopped 110 feet in therapy.
   He can count verbally to ten.
   He still does not have his leg brace.

7-17-86, Thursday
   Stan played cards—war and blackjack—with his friends. He has been showing signs of not knowing what kind of force he applies when interacting with and touching others. Louise asked Stan if he could feel the pressure when he needed to relieve himself in his bladder or bowels. He shook his head no. She asked him if he felt the warmth after he relieved himself. He shook his head no again, although his responses have not always been reliable lately. I wonder if he has been medically evaluated regarding this?

7-18-86, Friday
   Emil and I visited. Emil played blackjack with Stan. I sat beside Stan and watched, available to coach him if needed. It was not needed. He made his own decisions and I silently agreed with them. He got confused only once. It took a long time for him to decide, but his decisions were correct. He was not as tired or confused. The reduction of his medication is apparent.

Helen

It's interesting. I have played war and fish over the years more times than you could shake a stick at. The similarities are amazing. Always look around for the similarities in everything. They are there. It's no coincidence; it's by design. We attract *It*.

Bill

7-19-86, Saturday

Third weekend home. Stan has attended a party every weekend that he has come home. His first weekend home was a neighbor's picnic for the Fourth of July. The second weekend was Kevin's graduation party. For this, the third weekend, a neighbor is planning a surprise fiftieth birthday party for her husband, with a DJ and everything!

Stan's phenobarbital has been reduced by 30 mg each dose. He's now receiving:

Phenobarbital:	60 mg at 9:00 a.m.
	90 mg at 9:00 p.m.
Tegretol:	200 mg at 8:00 a.m., noon, 4:00 p.m.

7-20-86, Sunday

Emil notarized a letter Louise wrote to the judge on the driver's behalf. She wrote a plea for mercy/clemency, which she was sending to the driver's lawyer. She felt she could not get on the stand to testify without breaking down and it would hurt the driver's case. She also wanted the judge to know that she didn't want the driver punished for what happened. She sent a copy of the letter to her lawyer for approval before she actually sent it.

7-21-86

The lawyer called approving Louise's letter. He told her that the driver has been turned down for the ARD program that he had applied for. The Travises' lawyer is going to call the driver's lawyer to offer his services if there is any way he can help.

Stan's bill at Bryn Mawr from May 21 to June 30 will be twenty-two thousand to twenty-three thousand dollars. It is being paid by the CAT Fund.

Helen

On some of my bike rides in the French countryside in the region Midi-Pyrenees, department Haute Garonne, where there are many farmers cultivating the land and the land begins to roll toward the majestic mountains bordering Spain, I often pass by the Verdaich Clinic. When I see some of the patients outside, I usually ride my bike to them and chat a bit. They are head injury patients and seemed pleased that I and my American accent take some time for a visit and talk. I began doing this in 2010.

Bill

Louise was cleaning Stan's groin area from under the towel. He said, "Ooh" and showed signs of pain or discomfort on his face. Louise called Doc, who examined him and said he has a rash or fungus in the groin area. Doc applied Mycelog over the weekend and informed the nurse when he returned Stan to Bryn Mawr.

Louise and Doc were expecting guests around 3:00 p.m. Emil and I arrived at 2:00 p.m. Doc was outside working on the jeep. When Doc came in, he checked to see if all the preparations were complete for the couple's arrival. Louise assured Doc the table was set and all was ready, but they had to treat Stan's bedsore. Doc immediately became tense and started shouting, "Why didn't you call me? You knew it had to be done! Now, @#$(&, %&$#!" He came in and grabbed the wheelchair, cursing, and pulled Stan out of the room, cursing repeatedly. Doc also knows the bedsore must be treated three times a day. Because Doc had created such a whirlwind with his cursing and quick movements, I hoped that Stan was too confused to feel bad that his condition made these demands and stresses. Stan can't help it, and I only hoped he didn't feel bad or upset by this. I feel so bad for all of them. I know Doc is extremely tense, with just cause, and it is okay, but I also know how difficult it is for the rest of the family to live with this. These tirades and outbursts are difficult to handle, but they may be what saves Doc from a breakdown. It is a release valve for him. I just pray, Jesus, that you help the family and strengthen, comfort, and protect them during these times.

Helen

Grace is unmerited favor. It is a gift without you having to do anything for it or about it. Grace is how we did this.

Louise

Correct thinking is to imagine the idea and visualize it as already done. Imagine all the details of your picture. Create a perfect picture and an idea that is good and harmonious. Go to the silence regularly to commune with, to be with, to touch, to feel the maker, the one universal mind. Make each act perfect. Everything, every person will move toward you and you toward it, moving you closer to your goal. It's the law. Welcome to life!

I see this law every day in nature around my farms: The animals, the plants, the hills, and valleys. I observe, compare, contrast, analyze, and deduce. Everywhere I see *Its* growth and change. I smile and count my blessings. *It's* amazing!

Bill

7-21-86

Paul was teasing Stan about his girlfriend. Paul was hugging her. Stan took her arm and pulled her away. When he was unsuccessful using just his left arm, he also lifted his right arm and her with both arms. Stan said, "I said mine," referring to his girlfriend. Stan seemed agitated by this teasing.

Stan also played puff basketball with Paul. This was the first time he used his right arm. Slowly and with great effort he raised it to shoulder level, had it completely outstretched and with some wrist motion he threw the ball. Sometimes, while making this enormous effort he would drop the ball and lose it as he tried to get his arm up and stretched out. Louise said he did better with his arm playing with Paul than anything he has accomplished so far in therapy.

Louise was leaving church when a woman approached her. The woman, who was very emotional, said to her, "I don't know what to say to you that might help, but I thought it might help you to know that some of the boys that used to play Hatboro Horsham Little League with Stan when he was a child, have formed a prayer group to pray for him." Louise didn't even know the woman. Louise told her that she would like to know who the boys were so she could thank them. Louise also told me that when she went to be with the Lord, that he would allow her to see all those people that actually had been praying for Stan.

7-22-86

Stan seemed very tired again. Repeatedly, he said, "No," while nodding his head yes. After this happened several times Louise looked at him in the face and demonstrated, nodding her head up and down, and said, "Stan, this is yes." Then, shaking her head, she said, "This is no." He mixed these up for a long time.

The mother of another patient asked Stan for a hug. He hugged her with his left arm. She said that wasn't good enough. She wanted both arms. He looked at his right arm and tried lifting it up. Stan looked hopelessly at it and shook his head no. Louise reassured him by saying, "That's okay, you probably wore it out playing basketball with Paul yesterday."

Stan said, "Hi, David," when he arrived. It made David's day.

When we arrived Stan was napping. He was lying on his right side and his right hand was purple—almost black. I pointed this out to the nurse. She turned him and commented, "His circulation is rotten."

After dinner, Stan broke out in an allergic rash that was on his neck, torso, and face. He kept rubbing his eye. Louise showed the nurse and she said she would put some cream on it. The staff could not decide the cause of the rash.

Stan is now using a wheelchair that he can move himself. Louise asked him if he wanted to show me how he could move the chair, but he shook his head no. It's very difficult to do since he has to do it all with only his left arm and leg.

7-25-86

The podiatrist cut out Stan's ingrown toenail. When he is home on the weekend Louise will have to soak it twice a day, apply medication, and rewrap it. His nails were not cut in the hospital and they have grown over the ends of his toes. They were concerned he'd get an infection, which possibly could go into the bone in his shattered leg.

7-26-86

When we saw Stan his toe was wrapped. After therapy, we were waiting for Stan's medication that he was going to take home over the weekend. Louise asked if there were any follow-up instructions concerning the treatment of the ingrown toenail. The nurse did not know, but said she would check. Upon returning she gave Louise the instructions. Since she had not checked earlier, she had neglected to treat it that morning. It was already 2 p.m. She told Louise when she got him home to do it twice.

I went with Louise to pick up Stan to bring him home. He wasn't through with therapy yet. It was the first time I saw him use the walker, and he finally has his brace that makes walking easier. The brace is constructed in a bent position that allows Stan to touch the floor with his toe while the brace supports his weight, keeping it off the leg. This allows him to walk rather than hop. The walker is a typical one with an armrest attachment. He does, however, have difficulty getting his arm up high enough to lay it in the armrest. He needed help. After the arm is lying in the rest, there is a cylinder with a knob on top that he holds on to. He grasps it with his right hand.

When Louise arrived, Stan hugged her and got his right arm up high enough to complete the circle, touching it to his left arm.

7-27-86

Doc and Louise told Stan that Grandpop Cataldi died. He was upset and depressed the whole weekend.

Stan told David, "I walked!" Stan also stayed dry all weekend and used the urinal when Louise gave it to him.

7-28-86

As Louise, Mom, Stan, and his girlfriend were coming out of the Bryn Mawr, they noticed the basketball hoop outside the therapy department. They pointed to it for Stan. He shook his head no, that he couldn't see it. Mom was wearing a red skirt, so she went to the hoop and stood under the net. He shook his head that he didn't see it. His girlfriend, who was wearing fuchsia, ran to the hoop and jumped up and down, pointing to it. Stan indicated that he still couldn't see it. She asked if he could see her. He couldn't. She moved closer, asking if he could see her yet. He shook his head no. His girlfriend kept advancing and questioning him. He didn't firmly nod yes until she was about twenty feet away, and until she was that close, he kept shaking his head no, or was indefinite. We are not sure if he actually saw her or not.

Doc wants to take Stan to Wills Eye Hospital's neuro-ophthalmology unit for an evaluation and correction. Doc fears that his sight may be hampering his progress. Louise would rather put it off till the end.

Helen

My brother sustained a serious eye injury and was a patient at Wills Eye.

Bill

Stan had played basketball with another patient who'd been in Abington Memorial Hospital and whose family we tried to help at the time. We've remained in touch since then. I remember seeing this patient's mom a while later and being surprised how differently she (and we) looked without the stress of the trauma unit on our faces.

We've met some of the nicest people through all this.

Louise

7-31-86

Stan verbalized several names tonight: Joanne, David, Linda.

8-2/3-86, Weekend

We celebrated Kevin's birthday.

While driving Stan out to Bryn Mawr on Monday, Louise updated us about the weekend.

Louise had Stan on the commode and asked him if he had done anything. He said, "No." She kept checking and he kept saying, "No." She asked him if he was sure and he was sure that he had not used it. After much time and many "no" responses, she looked and he had in fact used it without even knowing it.

Louise asked Stan if he needed to use the urinal. He looked at her and definitely said, "No." She coaxed him to try. He became more assertive, and finally angry, saying, "NO," he did not need to use it. Within a few seconds after she gave up, it ran onto the floor and a look of disbelief came over his face. Stan reached out to her like a child to see if Louise was angry. She reassured him, and suggested that in the future he needed to be more patient with her also when she asks, and be more willing to try.

Louise said Stan has difficulty with top, bottom, left, and right.

Doc seemed distraught when speaking about Bryn Mawr releasing Stan. He feared it would slow his progress and he was ready to fight their logic on this point. Doc thought that it would be best for Stan if they have him stay or have daily outpatient physical therapy. He was incredulous at their thought. Usually when a patient is released he is able to return for outpatient therapy independently, thought Doc. These individuals can tell time, follow schedules, and know where to go. Stan can't do any of those things. Doc painted a picture of Stan being dropped off and just sitting there not knowing what to do or where to go. Doc laughed the bitterest laugh. It was such a cold laugh that it went right through me. He was probably crying out in pain.

Helen

CHAPTER FOUR
STRENGTH AND HAVING A PLAN

When we have the inspiration to create something and we can see it in its final form clearly and completely, we become a part of it and it becomes a part of us. It becomes extremely real to us. We give this all our attention, we concentrate on it, and we enter into the spirit of it, just like the seed in the ground reaching into the earth, to all the minerals, to grow. Life is good.

I once heard of a story about a young adult who seemed hopelessly destined to a life of despair. The doctors said the young adult would die a mentally, emotionally, spiritually, and physically crippled man, and that there was no hope for him. They had never seen a case like his cured. The young adult asked the doctors what they would do if he was their son. They said, "Don't listen to us. Look for a cure, move forward, and fight. As long as you are alive, continue to move forward and fight. No matter what, don't give in—move forward."

The young adult began saying a phrase to himself, day and night. It became such a part of him that it was on the tip of his tongue always. He wished health and happiness for everyone. He replaced fear with love and forgiveness. He began to search for a way to be of service to the world. This young adult has been cured. The doctors were speechless. Twenty-three years later, this person is a healthy man and living a life filled with family and friends, and is creating what he wants.

Bill

Music Therapy

8-4-86, Monday

Stan has begun the Casio music therapy. I asked him if he liked it and he smiled happily, saying, "Yeah."

Tegretol medication was decreased by 40 percent. He is no longer taking an 8:00 p.m. dose.

Stan played tic-tac-toe with Grandmom and he won. Kevin and Andy Dooley came to visit. Stan used his right hand to put some fruit on his spoon. He was slowly able to raise it to his mouth with his right arm.

Helen

Andy is a friend, neighbor, and former Bryn Mawr patient. Andy sustained a traumatic brain injury before Stan and is an inspiration to us. He has gone through some therapy with Stan.

Louise

8-5-86, Tuesday

Louise had Stan on the toilet. His penis started to pop up. He pushed it back down, which indicates he has feeling and sensation, even if only intermittent.

Stan's cousin, Cheryl, came with her son, Kevin, for a visit. Stan held Kevin on his lap using both arms.

Helen

Physical Therapy

8-6-86, Wednesday

At nine o'clock, I went to Stan's therapy with Louise. While there, Louise gave authorization for Stan to be photographed for a new Bryn Mawr brochure. The therapist put on a new brace and asked Stan if it pinched. Stan shrugged, seeming to indicate that he didn't know.

Using the walker, Stan put his arm in the armrest by himself and closed the Velcro over it. He used to need assistance getting it up to the armrest. Stan walked the entire length of the therapy room and out to the lobby. He selected an opening wide enough to pass through with the walker. He sidestepped until he was positioned in front of the seat, then he lowered himself into the seat. After resting, he repeated the entire process independently. He made it look easy. The therapist said he used to grit his teeth in pain while doing this. She was pleased how easy it seemed to be for him now.

Stan returned to the therapy department using the walker. The therapist instructed Stan to go to the raised mats. It's almost like a bed, with wooden sides and a plastic-covered mattress (mat) resting on it. He approached the mat at the corner. The therapist directed him to turn around and move up the side to the middle. He negotiated the walker around and all the way back to the side of the mat. Sidestepping, he moved to the middle of the side of the mat and then sat himself down. He then lay down, raising his own right leg up onto the mat. He used to need assistance getting his right leg up. A large plastic roll was placed under his knees. He raised his right leg more than twenty times! Next he raised his hips, tightening his buttocks. The therapist now is able to just tell Stan what to do and he does it. He used to need more help, demonstrations, etc. He now knows what is expected and understands and responds to verbal instructions. For example, "Raise left leg."

Stan's girlfriend has been on vacation this week. She drove up to surprise Stan. He kept looking at her and giggling. He was beside himself with joy.

Stan exercised his ankle, raising the toes on each foot. He is able to pull his toes up on the right foot. He has only recently begun to do this. He can't do it the full range, but it is a beginning. Using both feet, he is not yet able to separate the motion of moving toes up and down versus joining big toe to big toe.

Occupational Therapy

They took pictures of Stan's morning routine. The therapist asked Stan to put the pictures in sequence. They were numbered. The therapist explained that Stan currently needs motivation and stimulation for these functions. He needs to be told what to do next.

Picture #
1   Bare chest – applying deodorant
2 & 3 Putting shirt on – note, must put right arm in first
4   Toothpaste on brush
5   Brushing teeth
6   Washing face
7 & 8 Combing hair
9   Breakfast

The therapist said if given enough time he can dress himself except for shoes and socks. He can even pull his own pants on. Stan played the game Concentration by Milton Bradley, ages four to ten. The therapist took out nine pairs of cards and mixed them up, laying them facedown. Stan was instructed to turn two cards over and indicate if they matched. If they matched he kept the pair. If they did not match, they got turned over in their place facedown.

Stan was slow, easily distracted, and uninterested in the game. The therapist finally conceded and said, "One more turn." Stan sighed, turned over a pair, which did not match, and turned them back over again. He then glared at the therapist as if to see if she was going to keep her word and end the game. Stan only got one match.

Speech Therapy
Communication Disorders

Louise thought it would be too distracting if we all went in. Besides that, she feared it would embarrass him and he would be tense, since it is the most difficult area for him. Louise said they worked with pictures. They put one picture in front of Stan with a row of pictures above him. She said the pictures were tricky and detailed, and often facing a different direction. He had to find the matching picture. Sometimes he needed to mentally reverse the direction of the picture to determine the match.

Occupational Therapy

They took Stan to the apartment to discuss Louise's concerns regarding Stan's homecoming. Louise later came out and said we could join them. They were practicing tub transfers. The therapist said they could get bars that attach to the toilet seat rather than bars that go into the walls and the floor. Then, when Stan no longer needs them, they can just be removed. There is a seat that fits on both sides of the tub. Stan transferred himself from the wheelchair to the seat, although at home he'll probably be transferring himself using the walker. Stan transferred himself by standing, pivoting, holding on to the arm of the wheelchair, and then lowering himself to the seat. Next, he turned his bottom, lifted his left leg over the edge of the tub, then lifted his right leg partway and, using his hand, pulled it up the rest of the way to the edge and over. He did it with relative ease. I was impressed and applauded him. He reversed the process to get out. He pivoted his bottom toward the side, which meant his right leg was first to get over the edge. He tried unsuccessfully. He then tested if perhaps he could get his good left leg over first. He decided that wasn't possible. He repositioned himself on the seat facing toward the side even closer. This time, raising his right leg and assisting the rest of the way with his hand, he got it over, then followed with his left leg.

He looked at us like, "No big deal," as we cheered!

He stood, pivoted, and sat himself back in the wheelchair. It didn't seem like it was the first time he had done it. I was impressed with the thought processes as well as the way he maneuvered.

Helen

My life as an Ironman triathlete was like a science experiment to me. I was engrossed in it. It became a part of me and I became a part of it. For eighteen years it was life! Perhaps Stan was beginning to view his new life much in the same way. Perhaps he was beginning to have the fire, the passion, the focus, to do what was necessary to become whole again. With the love and support of people—many, many beautiful people—he was doing just that! He was growing the necessary brain cells to live, grow, and change, focusing on what he wanted!

Bill

Physical Therapy

Stan practiced walking the ramps in and out of the buildings. He also practiced walking on the grass.

Helen

I have many especially fond memories of being on the grass in my bare feet. You see, after a long endurance-oriented swim workout at the Phoenix Swim Club I'd practice transitions by jumping out of the pool, jogging to the grass track some one hundred meters away at the club, and running a cool eight hundred to twelve hundred meters. I'd love to feel the grass, dirt, and cement under my feet. I'd visualize coming out of the water in transition, heading toward my bike to be off on the bike leg of the event.

Bill

Speech Therapy

Since so much time was taken by the photos in the earlier session, the therapist set up another session and prepared an observation room for us to observe Stan. Stan said: *me, man, map, milk, mat*, and *moon*. He declined to say: *mile* and *meal*. The therapist had him match pictures. She commented that he paid good attention to shapes and detail. For the first two or three photos he had to find the one picture that matched the picture on top. For the next two or three he had to find two pictures that matched the one on top. He got all but one right.

The therapist asked Stan how old he was: thirteen, twenty, twenty-five, thirty, twenty-two? As she was getting close to his age (twenty-two), he said, "Close." She wrote twenty-five and twenty-two and asked him which. He pointed to twenty-two. She said twenty-two, but he didn't say yes. She told him that his records state he is twenty-two.

She asked him if his father was a truck driver. He nodded yes. Maybe he meant that his father has driven a truck? She then wrote *doctor* and *truck driver*. He pointed to *truck driver*. She asked him if he lived in Texas. He said, "Yes." She wrote *Texas* and *Pennsylvania* and he pointed to Texas. She wrote *Hatboro* and *Philadelphia* and asked him if he lived in Hatboro, and he said, "Yes."

Louise tried asking him if he knew the direction, but he didn't know.

8-7-86

Stan walked from the lounge in the rear of the building where he was eating dinner, all the way out to the elevator, down to the ground floor, through the hall, and outside to the wall.

8-13-86

The discharge date was extended to October 2.

8-16-86

Stan went to a Chinese restaurant.

8-17-86

What a difference in ten days! He could raise his right hand. I'm still amazed how he is able to dress himself. As I mentioned earlier, Stan follows the pictures that were taken and posted on the wall with Velcro to show him what to do and in what sequence.

Louise took him around through the day, asking him at every turn which direction to take — for example, to the elevator. He still consistently does not know.

Stan used only the walker all weekend. He did not use the wheelchair. He drank holding his glass in his right hand. When shaking hands with his right hand he could not let go.

Helen

We can't possibly see, think, and imagine what the creative intelligence is sending our way for the good of what we want to accomplish. Like a practically blind bowler bowling a perfect game, we have to appreciate what focus, faith, trust, persistence, failure, and growth went into that perfect night during the previous days, weeks, months, and years.

Bill

One time I used his bathroom after he had finished. He hadn't flushed and his urine mixed with the water in the toilet bowl looked like tea. I went out to the nurses' station and found Dr. Long. At first they thought it was from his meds. I now think it was the onset of the hepatitis C he got from all the blood he had received.

8-18-86

They took Stan off Tegretol (anti-seizure med). It was affecting his liver function. Perhaps it was the hepatitis C that was affecting his liver function. He is much brighter and he even skipped his nap. His responses were usually appropriate.

8-25-86

Neuro-Ophthalmologist

"Your sight may or may not come back, Stan; but it would take a really long time."

I was so upset when they told me I fought the tears and couldn't talk about it with the nurses when we returned. I remembered a young man who was in Abington Memorial Hospital at the same time as Stan whose family had told me that he lost the sight in one eye. I was so upset for him and now, along with everything else, Stan can't see out of his left eye. We later discovered that he'd lost part of the sight or had huge field cuts in the right eye, leaving him with only about one-quarter of his total vision.

Louise

They had difficulty with this exam due to his speech trouble. The third nerve in his left eye might have been damaged. It might be blind. I was so disappointed. When I spoke to Louise, I told her that I had heard that the examination didn't go well. Louise responded, "No, to the contrary." I asked her how she thought it was good news. She said it was what she needed to hear because she couldn't bear another surgery. I hoped something could be done to restore his sight and therefore I had interpreted the news as bad news. She explained that God has to do a lot of work before she could handle that and she was hoping that eventually it would come back.

8-28-86

Stan can count to one hundred. He missed the seventies.

8-30-86

Doc was bragging about how well Stan was doing in therapy. Stan knows where his eyes, nose, and so on are.

9-6-86

Doc had difficulty accepting Stan's blindness. He put Stan through all kinds of eye tests to prove to himself that he was blind in that eye. Stan's brother Kevin said he watched and it was the first time he cried.

Stan did not want to believe it and Doc would not believe it.

9-18-86

We were all eating lunch with Kevin. Stan pushed himself away from the table and started moving his chair toward his room. Kevin followed, questioning Stan. He asked Stan if he had to go to the bathroom. Stan said, "Thank you." Kevin helped him and he did go. This was the first sign of feeling and knowing that he had to go! Praise God, that's a biggie.

9-24-86

Discharge now extended to November 6, the day before Stan's birthday. Bryn Mawr said he would benefit from a longer stay. He needs a change, though, which would stimulate and motivate him in other areas. Stan is gaining sensation and control of his bladder. No wet laundry all week! Stan got up in the middle of the night and walked to the bathroom without his brace.

10-3-86

Orthopedic Appointment

Stan was told to come back in two months. He was directed to continue using the brace and walker. Louise was told not to panic if he walks to the bathroom without the brace.

10-14-86

Stan was so tired that he fell asleep standing up. They had to skip two therapies.

Physical Therapy

The therapists are working on the stairs with Stan. Using crutches, he puts the crutch on one side and holds the rail with his other hand. He ascended fifteen steps the first time he tried. They are using the crutches to slowly replace the walker.

He is so tired from the phenobarbital.

Helen

Planning and Scheduling Strategies

This is what Stan uses to fill his five pillboxes for the week. The pill bottles are on a tray and each bottle has a picture of the pill on the top for easy identification. When we replace the bottle with a new one, we just transfer the cap.

Notice that there is a picture of each pillbox under what time of day they are for and where that pillbox is kept. You'll also see yellow dotted lines with the word *check* written on it. When he reaches that line, he knows to stop and self-check that it is correct by passing it to whoever is working with him. If it's okay, Stan continues to complete the filling and checks again.

The p.m. box has a blue box rubber banded to the bottom of it with his Lactaid pills in it, so he has them with him at all times if needed.

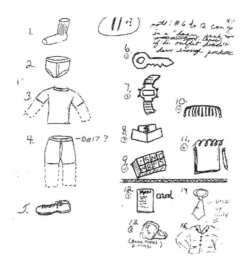

This is a numbered list of items he needs to gather and take to the bathroom for his grooming. It's on the black box that he keeps his pocket things in when not on his person. A list of his current medications is on the blue box, too. It's located on the large night table at the foot of his bed.

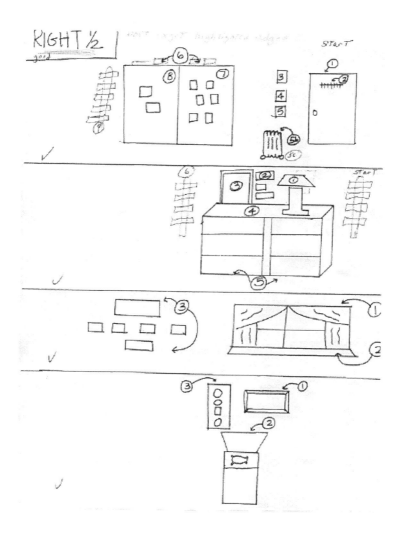

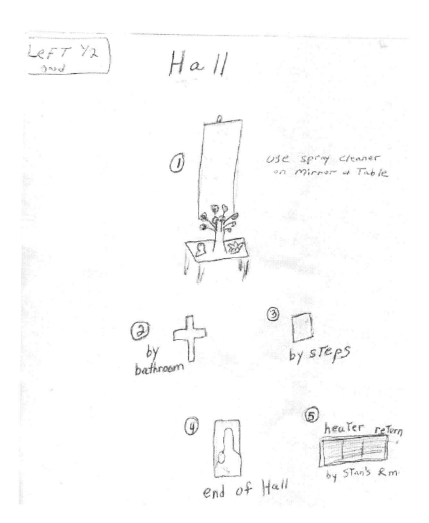

Left ½ end

Hall

① use spray cleaner on mirror + Table

② by bathroom

③ by steps

④ end of Hall

⑤ heater return by Stan's Rm.

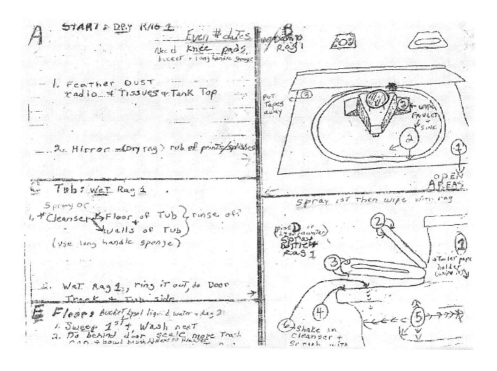

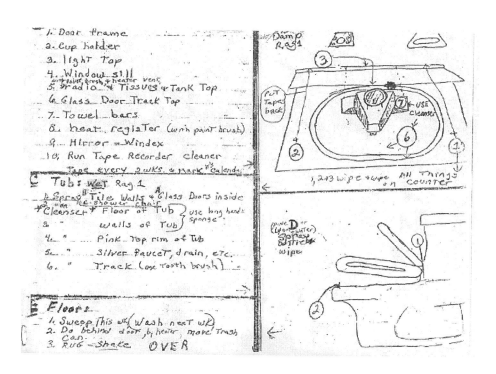

1. Door frame
2. Cup holder
3. light Top
4. Window sill
5. radio & Tissues & Tank Top   spray paint brush + heater vent
6. Glass Door Track Top
7. Towel bars
8. heat register (w/ pain brush)
9. Mirror - Windex
10. Run Tape Recorder cleaner
    Tape every 2 wks. & mark calendar

C. Tub: WET Rag 1
1. Spray Tile Walls & Glass Doors inside   A   on the shower chair
*Cleanser + Floor of Tub} use long hand
3.   "   walls of Tub} sponge
4.   "   Pink Top rim of Tub
5.   "   Silver Faucet, drain, etc.
6.   "   Track (use Tooth brush)

E. Floors
1. Sweep This wk (Wash next wk)
2. Do behind door, by heater, move Trash
   Can.
3. RUG - Shake   OVER

Damp Rag

PUT Tape back

USE Cleanser

1, 2, 3 wipe + wipe   All Things on Counter

(use D or lysol + water) Spray & Trick wipe

Keeping it Simple

No two brain injuries and therefore strategies are alike. Keep it simple. These were the words of Stan's neuropsychologist. Too much verbal or visual information makes it more difficult for Stan to sort through and then process the information.

One of the successes Louise has had with Stan is what she calls visual spatial. She writes up his strategies and spaces them — in other words, sections them. When he completes a section, Stan goes back and checks it off. He lacks initiative as a result of his injury and this forces him to circle back and do an edit. The strategies are easy to understand and she uses stick figures for Stan when possible. She also uses different colors to group things together; to distinguish one from the other.

Stan has his strategies in sheet protectors and uses erasable markers and crayons to check off what he has done.

Louise divides some bigger, more detailed, more time-consuming jobs in half since it is too much for him to focus on. For example, when he cleans his room, he does one half thoroughly while he only touches up the other half. He marks this on his calendar on his bedroom door and keeps a loose-leaf binder. The next week he reverses it. This is the same procedure Stan uses for cleaning the bathroom, which has even number dates and odd number dates. The bathroom instructions have a reversible sheet protector that he puts up on the medicine cabinet for convenient use.

Stan keeps a logbook, which Louise refers to as his memory. It reminds him of all the things he needs to do and he records all he does in it. He also tracks his monthly pay, gym attendance, bowling scores, etc. For his daily activities, he carries a pocket-size card in plastic which has his schedule on it. He has one for each day of the week. It tells him what he needs to do; he does it, writes it in his logbook, crosses it off with the same colored marker, and proceeds to the next thing.

Stan has a checklist for grooming in the bathroom and another that he must carry with him at all times. He has a five-by-seven card he uses when he fills his pillboxes that shows him what goes in where for each day. For grocery shopping, he uses index cards that are itemized per card. It has a picture of the item, what aisle it's in, and how many he has to get. They are held together with a ring.

There are strategies pertaining to appliances, clocks, microwaves, answering machines, alarm clocks, and so forth as well. Louise puts a colored tape next to the on/off or function area of the item. She uses the traffic light theme, putting red tape for *off* and green tape for *on*, for example. Blue or yellow tape is used for another setting.

For his job at the supermarket, he has an entire loose-leaf book divided with tabs according to the tasks he must complete. He has a canvas tote bag he keeps in his work locker with all the supplies and strategies he uses to do his job. There is also a list of everything that goes into the bag.

Every brain injury is different and therefore every strategy is unique. The key is to find what works, be creative, and keep it simple.

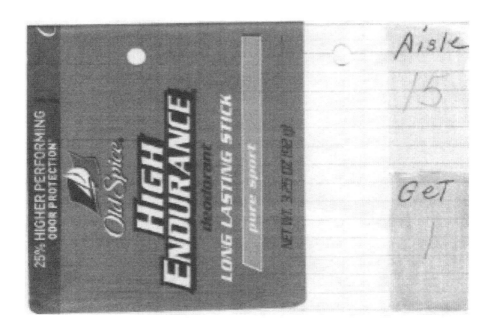

CHAPTER FIVE

POWER AND BEING
YOUR OWN PERSON

Homecoming

11-6-86, Discharge

Homecoming! We are all so excited about Stan's homecoming. Lawson's Flower Shop made big yellow ribbons that we put on our shrubs. Stan's friend made a Welcome Home sign on a four-feet-by-eight-feet piece of plywood, with streamers and flags on each side reaching down to the ground. This huge sign was installed on our front lawn.

I bought a roll of yellow plastic which most might use as a tablecloth. I cut it into strips, and Stan's friend and I tied them around every speed limit sign, pole, and street sign on both sides of Maple Avenue from County Line Road to Easton Road (Route 611), a distance of about one mile. We tied them all over our weeping cherry tree (a takeoff on the Tony Orlando and Dawn song, "Tie a Yellow Ribbon Round the Ole Oak Tree"). Neighbors knew of our expected return and waited by the sign to cheer and welcome him home.

Helen drove up and saw the display; she said it brought tears to her eyes. She couldn't get over the countless yellow ribbons lining the route home. The article and photos about Stan's homecoming were front and center, overtaking that year's election news. Stan's story appeared on the front page of the local paper!

Stan's birthday is November 7. We invited family and friends to celebrate the birthday he almost didn't have. That entire night we played the song, "Tie a Yellow Ribbon," over and over again. Doc restarted the cuckoo clock that we had stopped the night of the crash, February 26, 1986. I briefly recalled what was happening that night: Stan had died once and had surgery; we were being informed of his second death and another surgery, and that perhaps it was time to think about donating his organs. That was the night that our hearts stopped as well. Starting the cuckoo clock, we were ready to climb the next mountain during the next phase of our lives.

That night Stan went on a double date. They "parked" at the air base. The night prior to discharge, Bryn Mawr gave him a T-shirt that had "Bryn Mawr Graduate" on it, and we had a pizza party with the other patients and staff in the brain injury unit.

Louise

Whenever we come to a crossroads, we can always stop and ask for directions. Commune with nature, be silent, and the answer will come. Be aware. The answers will come in many different shapes and sizes. Visualize what you want. Make it perfect. Go get it! Do it! Focus on the good and what you are already thankful for. It'll happen. Have faith. Life is good! Anything is possible!

Bill

11-23-86

Stan formulated his own sentence spontaneously. He said, "Mom, I want to tell you something." Louise reacted so excitedly when he said it that he laughed at her reaction and forgot what he wanted to say. His next sentence was, "Mom, come over here!"

In church he said the Our Father and some of the responses. He got 100 percent in Speech Therapy on Friday. During his Cognitive Therapy session he worked with a computer. Stan did well. He beat the computer on the majority of the games. This was a week of continued advancement for him.

Helen

I made up a flyer and sent it to family, friends, Stan's medical team, and everyone involved in his care. We had a Mass of Thanksgiving at St. Joseph's, our church in Warrington, Pennsylvania. Monsignor Peck said the mass. St. Joseph's and St. Catherine of Sienna's music groups joined together to play the music during the mass. The women's group from church brought refreshments which were available to everyone in the church hall after mass. Many attendees brought cake and refreshments as well. Friends were kind enough to direct parking. The church was filled to capacity with over four hundred people.

We had the squeeze ball Stan used in the intermediate unit in the hospital brought up to the altar at the offertory along with the gifts, and my husband spoke. Two of the doctors that attended told me they were so emotional from it all that they went out afterward to settle down and talk about Stan's recovery.

The mass book and readings were filled with the scriptures the Lord had filled me with during Stan's hospital and rehabilitation stays, as well as the readings that had filled me when I was at mass during that time.

Louise

Please join us as we celebrate the
miracle of STan Travis III at a

MASS OF

THANKSGIVING

DEC. 3 7:30 P.M.

ST. JOE'S Loc. County Line Rd
& RT. 611

Pass it along. ALL who prayed or supported
me in any way are welcome.

Prelude: THAT'S WHAT FRIENDS ARE FOR

(This is what we have found in you and what we hope we can be for you.)

(Please Stand)

Entrance Hymn: THIS IS THE DAY THE LORD HAS MADE

Greetings

(After the entrance song, all make the sign of the cross.)

Priest.

In the name of the Father, and of the Son , and of the Holy Spirit.

All: Amen.

Priest: The grace of our Lord Jesus Christ and the love of God and the fellowship of the Holy Spirit be with you all.

All: And also with you.

Penitential Rite

All: I confess to almighty God, and to you , my brothers and sisters, that I have sinned through my own fault in my thoughts and in my words, in what I have done , and in what I have failed to do; and I ask blessed Mary, ever virgin, all the angels and saints, and you my brothers and sisters, to pray for me to the Lord our God.

First page of the Mass booklet

The entrance hymn at Stan's mass was "This Is the Day the Lord Has Made." This is the same song that was the theme song at a life-changing retreat I attended in the early 1990s.

Just as Stan was focused on healing himself, I was similarly focused on triathlon. In fact, I continued to train even during the retreat. I snuck out of the retreat house where I was sleeping to go for a run. I did this all three days between 3:00 a.m. and 5:00 a.m.

Right or wrong, we were acting with a definite purpose in mind!

Bill

Stan will be going to Bryn Mawr for outpatient therapy. Transportation and an aide were arranged. I eventually got back to my prayer meetings on my "mental health night."

Trying to do everything really got to me. We had a family meeting about my need for help and decided to hire a cleaning person. At one point I lay across the bed and cried and cried. It came out in spurts, just like I seemed to acquire it, like it had been pushed down inside me and continued to be pushed down over time. I couldn't stop crying. I realized later that I had cut myself off from all my support systems—I had amputated myself, so to speak. I could no longer go to daily mass and communion after Stan came home, for example. I couldn't go to my prayer meetings and be with my friends with whom I could talk or vent. I had backed off from them and they thought I had my hands so full and was busy. They didn't want to bother me.

I was told that eight to ten years post trauma things would be the worst. I couldn't help but wonder that if it was this bad now, what would years eight, nine, and ten be like. I remember saying, "Goody, goody, goody, I can't wait!" with such a sarcastic tone. Thank God that I continued to adjust, grow in the Lord, and lean on him. It did get better.

Louise

Family Day
Dave's first year at Philadelphia College of Medicine
1987

You never know what the universe is preparing for you. "Hold on, put your hand in ours and don't let go. We don't want to lose you," I remember hearing once.

Acknowledge how you feel. Feel it. Then let it go. Trust, trust, trust. Have faith. The situation has to get better if we continue to want to grow, change, or grow in acceptance, and move forward toward what we want. The universe, God, the energy, call *It* what you like, will sweep us along in that direction because that's the way life is. *It* always gets better. Good always triumphs. Good is all there is. Give your attention to where you want to be (the unconditional) and not where you are now (the condition). Experience teaches us that this is life.

Bill

12-5-86, Friday

We went to the orthopedic surgeon who x-rayed Stan's leg. The leg looks as healed as it'll be. It's not 100 percent, but good. Stan was given the directive that there could not be any contact sports. He no longer needed the walker or crutches, maybe just a cane. Dr. Sweterlitsch went on to explain that he hates to use plates. He said that problems usually develop with the plate or the screws and that they could break.

12-9-86, Tuesday

Kevin taught Stan to go to the bathroom "like a man." This is something only a guy can teach a guy. Women just don't get it.

Stan went into the bathroom alone and locked the door. He has been going to the bathroom by himself and seems quite proud of his independence. He was in there for a considerable length of time. Louise went to the door and asked him if he was all right. He said, "Yes." She left him alone a little longer, then went to the door again and asked him if he was done. Stan said, "Yes." Louise asked if he needed help and he responded, "Yes." She asked him to open the door. He didn't open it. With a screwdriver they popped the lock and found him having a full-blown seizure. The TV was so loud that Louise didn't hear anything. His finger was scraped and he was confused and disoriented.

Later, when asked if he had a headache, he said, "Yes." Louise said that the first thing she did when she got to him was to check the side of his head to see if the shunt was working properly.

Stan's girlfriend called him in the evening. He very emotionally kept telling her that he loved her. After they had spoken for a while, she said it was late and she had to go to bed. Stan pleaded with her, "No! No! No!" Again with a lot of emotion, he repeated, "I love you!" She would respond, "I love you, too. It's getting late, though, and I have to go." Again he interrupted her with, "No! No! No! I love you." Finally, she asked to speak with Louise. She explained what had been happening. Louise discussed it with Stan. She said she knew there was something Stan wanted to tell her, so how about they let her hang up since it was getting late and that she (Louise) would try to help him find the words. If they were able to verbalize what he wanted to tell his girlfriend they could call her back. Stan agreed. Louise questioned Stan and made all kinds of suggestions trying to determine what he wanted to tell her.

Stan was increasingly frustrated. Finally, Louise asked, "Did you want to ask her to marry you?" Stan responded with glee, happily laughing and clapping his hands, "Yes!" Louise rehearsed with him how to say it. They called her back and Stan asked her to marry him. Louise was overcome with emotion watching her son's love and joy.

12-10-86

The next morning Stan had a full-blown seizure. His aide was shaving him when it began. They called an ambulance and took him to Abington. Everyone was distraught.

Doc said that although it was his forty-eighth birthday, he felt like it was his eighty-fourth. "Episodes like this feel like they age you," he said. Doc went on to explain that they will not be able to leave Stan alone at any time. Someone is going to have to be with him constantly. Louise began crying. She said they had just celebrated the Mass of Thanksgiving and everything was looking so good. She wondered why this was happening. Louise said she felt like a puppy dog that the Lord was training. She felt like she was on a very short leash.

The hospital did another CAT scan. I asked Doc how it looked. "Terrible!" Louise explained that it didn't show any additional damage and it just has not looked good since the trauma, and now everything was taking a turn for the worse. They don't know the reason for the seizure, but his phenobarbital level had dropped below the therapeutic level.

2-8-87

There was another seizure that was even scarier. When it was over, Stan had lost his speech and his right side. The seizure lasted about fifteen minutes. An ambulance was called and he was taken to the hospital again. They took an EEG that showed he had seizure activity in many parts of his brain. The phenobarbital was 15.5, within the therapeutic limits. Fifteen to thirty is considered a therapeutic level. They did another liver test to check the enzymes (liver function).

Stan's AST test was 115. Normal is between two and twenty-five. His ALT test was 199. Normal is between five and thirty-five.

Results of these blood tests

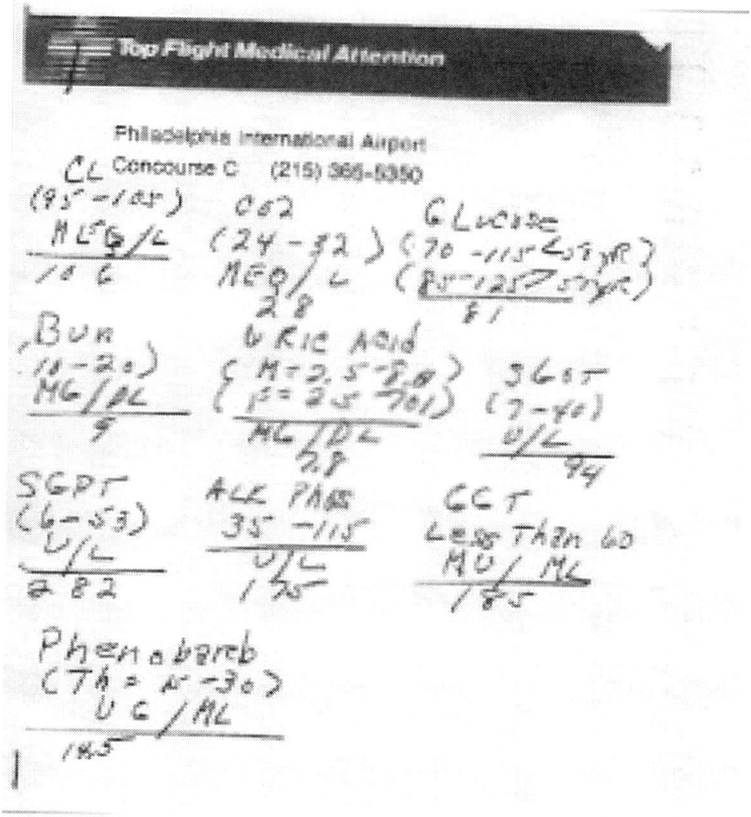
Top Flight Medical Attention

Philadelphia International Airport
Concourse C (215) 365-5350

CL
(95-105)
MEQ/L
106

CO2
(24-32)
MEQ/L
28

GLUCOSE
(70-115 <55 YR)
(85-125 > 55 YR)
81

BUN
(10-20)
MG/DL
9

URIC ACID
(M = 3.5-8.0)
(F = 2.5-7.0)
MG/DL
2.8

SGOT
(7-40)
U/L
94

SGPT
(6-53)
U/L
282

ALK PHOS
35-115
U/L
175

GGT
LESS THAN 60
MU/ML
185

Phenobarb
(TH = 10-30)
UG/ML
18.5

Note: Louise has all Stan's blood work charted.

2-20-87

Stan had a mini seizure in therapy. They are continuing to increase the phenobarbital.

Helen

I tried to stay with him constantly, going into the room across the hall to do other work while still keeping an eye on him. But, it was impossible for me to be with someone constantly and it was starting to drive me crazy. I got some nursery monitors to put around the house so that I could keep tabs on him from a distance. The monitors enabled me to hear the snorting and breathing changes of a seizure. The monitors made the sounds louder. I put some small wind chimes on his doorknob so I could hear if he got up and left his room. I also put a night light in the hallway and a gate at the top of the stairs.

Louise

3-3-87

The gastroenterologist, Dr. Anne Saris, suggested taking Stan off the medication that he is presently taking for his skin. It sometimes has side effects that show up like this. They are taking a blood test every other week to see if any improvement is indicated. If not, there is the possibility that he may have contracted hepatitis from the blood he received (non-A, non-B type hepatitis). This type of hepatitis cannot be tested through blood work, but rather would require a liver biopsy. They would approach it conservatively at first, ruling out the medication side effects. Initially they were going to do the blood work weekly, but Louise explained that his veins are in bad shape since his hospital stay and they often have to dig for them. Due to this discussion, the decision was made to do the blood work every other week.

I asked Louise how much blood he had received. She responded, "Eighteen to nineteen units."

Louise asked how he could have received contaminated blood. They explained that the screening picks up antibodies. However, if the donor had just contracted the hepatitis (or whatever) before the donation, the antibodies would not have been formed yet. The blood work is going to be done at Bryn Mawr since Stan probably wouldn't let anyone else do it. Note: There is no cure for hepatitis C.

3-4-87

Stan had another appointment with the orthopedic surgeon today. No brace and no cane! Stan's steps are normal. He doesn't take one at a time, but rather compensates by leading with the good leg (up) and then (down) with the bad leg. His next visit will be in four months. Dr. Sweterlitsch explained that, as long as the plate remains the bone will not heal as strong as it originally was, and that if they leave the plate in, the bone could snap just above the plate. When the plate is removed the bone will continue to heal and strengthen, filling in the holes from the screws. It will all be stronger if the plate comes out, and will also minimize the chances for emergency surgery in the event that something went wrong with the plate or screws.

Helen

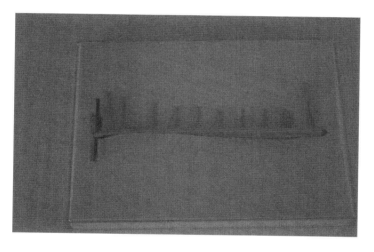

In February 1986, Stan's bone was so strong that Dr. Sweterlitsch went through several drill bits when installing the plate and screws.

Louise

The very essence of who we are always heals us if we get out of the way and let the process just happen. The power (God) that filled the holes in his bone with the new strong bone bond, is the same power that exists in sunflowers reaching for the sky, horses scratching each other's back, a warm embrace between lovers, a father holding hands with and smiling at his daughter, the seasons changing, a person changing an unhealthy life situation such as an addiction, and a bowler bowling a perfect game.

The answer is inside us—in the silence. Connect with *It*, feel *It*, breathe *It*, do *It*. We can be what we will ourselves to be. I've seen the practice of these thoughts bring people to their knees. For some, they explain that it raises the hair on their arms. Others get that shot of energy originating from their gut shooting up their back toward their neck. For some, this is their explanation of that powerful jolt they receive when connecting with the infinite. *It*'s just pure peace and joy.

Bill

Louise asked the doctor if Stan would need blood again, since they are now facing hepatitis issues or possible contamination from the blood. He said he probably won't need blood for that surgery, but as a precaution, Stan could give his own blood ahead of time. They probably wouldn't need more than two units.

Louise also asked about the concern of clots and bone infection. He said that the risk was one hundred times less than his first surgery, and under the circumstances bone infection was not an issue. Louise then asked about Stan being able to put weight on his leg after the surgery. The doctor said he would need crutches for six weeks.

3-7-87

Stan had another mini seizure. He felt it coming on. Stan said, "Uh, okay, trouble!" Louise asked him if it was a seizure and he answered, "Yes!" After the seizure, through questioning, he told Louise that he knew he was going to have a seizure because his eyes were beginning to "jump." Stan knows this to be true by experience; however, nobody can notice this by looking at him.

Stan had already told Louise that the seizures are scary for him. We can see that he is scared. Louise tried talking about it with him in the hope of calming his fears. She asked him what he feared. Stan replied, "To die." Louise reassured him that although it was scary, she had never heard (at that time) anyone dying from a seizure. He said, "Coma!"

Louise is having his hearing and ears checked. His hearing seems impaired on the right side of the shunt. Oh, good news! His range of hearing is okay. The problem is Stan's ability to process.

Helen

I started keeping a seizure log in case it would reveal some patterns or triggers, to let the doctors know what is going on, and to observe what they question. I also keep charts and a calendar about the seizures. I'm now on my fourth book.

When Stan was having seizure activity (misfirings, mini seizures, or internal shaking), I often lay beside him with my arm over him so I could feel if he started shaking. After a while, I just could not stay awake any longer "in case." I used to think I was handling things well, and then I'd get a tick or a twitch in my eye and I'd have to admit, I guess I'm not doing as well as I thought.

Once it was established that Stan had a seizure disorder, we no longer would take him to the hospital. We have oxygen at home. We were told to bring him, however, if they last a long time, if he has several close together, or if he doesn't seem to come out of one and then has another immediately. Dr. Long, his neurologist at Bryn Mawr, sent Stan to see Dr. Sperling at the Epilepsy Center in Philadelphia. Dr. Sperling suggested to "push through" his activity instead of letting them (the misfirings and headaches) interfere.

Stan has alien hand and leg syndrome, which is when his arms and legs move without him asking them to do so. It's almost like they have a mind of their own. He has several different types of misfirings and activities.

Concerns over his liver and possible damage to it continued. A liver biopsy was done by Dr. Anne Saris at AMH. I had to stay with him during and after because Stan needed to remain still for many hours. He has hepatitis C. They used to diagnose hepatitis A and hepatitis B and lump all the rest as non-AB. Now they diagnose hepatitis C, D, E, F, G, and H separately. The medical community has verified this.

6-23-87

We had our twenty-fifth wedding anniversary. I knew if it went by without a celebration, I'd be sorry. We drove to Cape Cod, not wanting to go too far away in case Stan got in trouble with surgeries or something.

We had a mass at our home with a dear monsignor family friend saying the service. Friends and family attended and then we headed to Meryl's restaurant. That night, when Stan's girlfriend said good-bye, there was something strange in it. I got a funny feeling. As it turned out, it really was "good-bye." I later found out she was seeing someone else and they eventually married. It was one of the hardest things I've ever had to tell Stan. In her absence, I'd call his friends to come visit him so he wouldn't have his evenings empty. After I told him, one night he wanted to cry but wasn't able to. I held him for a long time.

Later, we went to a wedding for a couple in his group of friends. Her new boyfriend was in the wedding party. They were considerate of Stan and didn't act like a couple. Their song (that of Stan and his former girlfriend), "Endless Love," was played at the reception and I lost it. I went to the ladies' room so no one would see how upset I was.

I don't think their romance was deliberate; it was just something that happened. It was a heartbreaker nonetheless, and very awkward when our paths would cross. I don't hold it against them. In hindsight, it was probably for the best. Marriages rarely survive in head injury cases. She was there for him during his hospitalization and rehabilitation, and her presence motivated him to fight. She did her job for Stan and I'm thankful for that. If they would've married, had children, and divorced, it would have been even harder for him. We are blessed that he is okay with his life now and enjoys people.

We'd drive past her street on the way to one of his doctors' offices and I'd pray we'd get the green light. If a red light stopped us, he'd point and say her name. I'd cringe whenever their song came on. As time has passed, Stan and I have spoken about the ins and outs of relationships, marriage, and children. Now that he sees this, he says, "Single" in a way affirming that he sees there is something to be said for being single. He has seen both of his brothers divorce. It was a challenge for Stan to get to this point — mentally, emotionally, and spiritually — but he has arrived.

Louise

Life is what we do with *It*.

Bill

Early on I'd hope that a nurse or therapist would see the person Stan is and fall in love with him. Then my thoughts turned to hoping he'd meet another patient and they'd fall in love. As I thought about it realistically, they'd both have their own deficits and needs. They might have to live with us for help, which could be a problem. They'd want the independence they couldn't have and children they couldn't raise on their own. Perhaps I'd over-extend myself and maybe they would resent me because they needed my help. It probably wouldn't work, and a divorce could be unbearable. If it happens, it happens, I thought. I no longer "look" for it for him. Once again he seems happy and content with his life. Maybe not 100 percent. but how many people are? It was hard for Stan when all his friends were getting married and he'd ask, "What about me?"

Louise

10-8-87

AMH ran an ad in the *Philadelphia Inquirer*. It was a message from the trauma team at the hospital. The piece told Stan's story and gave some statistics about the victims the team treats. It stated that over three-quarters of the traffic victims they treated the previous year had not been wearing their seat belt. The article went on to say that Stan was getting another chance, but not everybody does.

Note: Stan walked into the AMH ER days earlier and thanked each of the staff, one-on-one, for what they did for him.

Newspaper article

11-1-88

Doc recently spoke at AMH. The director of development wrote Doc a letter expressing the hospital's many thanks to him for sharing Stan's story. The author of the letter wrote that the audience to which Doc presented was deeply moved, had lumps in their throats, and some were on the verge of tears. The writer praised Doc for courageously presenting to quite a large audience on such an emotional topic.

Thank you letter to Doc

11-10-88

Doc received a letter from a doctor of proctology who had shared a table with him and his family at a recent dinner in Abington. This doctor said that he and his wife were moved by Stan's story and wanted to wish Doc and his family the very best going forward.

Appreciation letter to Doc

9-18-89

Doc received a letter from a minister and friend of the family. Doc had written a letter some time before to update the minister on Stan's progress. The writer of the letter was expressing his disbelief in what he was looking at in a local newspaper dated August 11, 1989. Stan Travis was water-skiing! The minister stated what he was looking at with words like miraculous comeback, perseverance, courage, family support, faith, and love.

Response to Doc's letter

A former patient of Doc's remembered the extra steps Doc took when treating him for an underactive thyroid. This patient described how Doc wrote letters to his insurance company to solve a problem. He remembered that Doc did not have to do this. The patient realized that Doc is a man who cares deeply for his patients and shows a great love for man in general.

Bill

Before the crash, while Stan was working at the Jenkintown Acme store, he would go back to the Baderwood store to visit. While talking to his co-workers he would bag customer orders for the cashiers, automatically. This is Stan!

After the crash, his brother Kevin worked at the Warrington Acme, and he spoke with management about hiring Stan there. They agreed. I took him there, met with the assistant manager, and filled out an application for him. On December 29, 1989, they hired him. He has continued to work with Acme until now: twenty-two years. He works at the New Britain/Chalfont store. He has to have a job coach with him to help him do his job. He can only work four hours per week. If he worked more, his performance would decline. Acme has been excellent to work with.

A dear friend of ours, Jack Street, got a liver transplant in Pittsburgh, and my husband had frequent contact with the transplant team. He asked them if Stan needed a liver transplant down the road, would the hepatitis C affect the new transplanted liver. They said yes. That wasn't, of course, the answer we wanted to hear, although we hoped he'd never need one. As time went on and concerns over liver blood tests and liver damage grew, Dr. Saris spoke to us about giving Stan interferon shots. I was concerned that the cost of the shots would push him over his annual cap with the Pennsylvania CAT Fund. I contacted the union and explained the whole thing. They agreed to cover the costs of the shots, which were at the time about six hundred dollars per prescription refill.

The shots were hard on Stan. He'd get flu-like symptoms, a fever, chills, aches and pains, and huge, swollen, red-hot, crater-like areas four to five inches in diameter at the injection site. These didn't go away before it was time for next shot. Therefore, another spot had to be used. As time passed, it was more and more difficult to find an area for the shot. He'd be just about getting over the reactions to the previous shot when it was time for the next.

They did baseline tests on Stan and after a time period checked him to see if he was responding. He was, so they continued with the shots per the treatment plan. The serum had to be refrigerated, so when we went somewhere we carried them in an insulated bag with cold packs. After completing his interferon shots, he was retested. The results were as if he had never gotten the shots. The tests were as bad as they were before all the shots. It really blew my mind and I was so bummed. Ever since the accident, I was expecting a miracle, but didn't think I needed to chase one or travel the world over for it. I felt that if the Lord or the Blessed Mother were going to give us healing they could do it right where we were. People would give me blessed oils and holy water, relics, or medals which we would use.

The leader of my prayer group and friend, Mary Messner, called me one day. She was on her way to visit someone in the hospital to bless them with oil she had received. The oil oozed out of a picture of the Sacred Heart of Jesus in the home of a visionary in the Philippines. She stopped by, we anointed Stan, we prayed, and she went on her way. I gave it no further thought. The time for Stan's regular blood work rolled around and we had it done. The results were good, and I didn't understand it. The results went from bad to good with absolutely no changes made. No change in medication or diet. Nothing was different. Then I remembered the oil that we blessed him with. I was almost afraid to think it, and certainly was reluctant to say it. Could it be?

Louise

The greatest power is the knowledge of our power. When we are willing to accept that our will, our power, is one and the same as the universal, then we can become one with it. We do this by being silent, still, and quiet. We look around and see it everywhere and all the time in the conditions that show up in our lives. We see it in nature. When we accept this, we have given up the need to control our life and the results.

Be patient with ourselves. Have faith and trust that all is well. Often, the troubles we experience will take care of themselves when we show this power of patience and being grateful—now.

Use this power to create. Be silent. Seek the inspiration. God gave life to us. What we do with *It* is our gift to him.

Bill

CHAPTER SIX

HAPPINESS IS A CHOICE - IT'S AN ATTITUDE AND BEING GRATEFUL

Animals are spontaneous. They follow their instincts and seem to always have the pleasure of being alive. *It's* who they are. How often do we take the time to really observe nature and become a part of *It*? Dogs, horses, and cats seem to always enjoy what they are doing. Stan and I love the water. I have communed with fish. I have been like a dolphin leaping through the surf during triathlons—just doing the action, happily.

When we realize that who we are is not connected to a result, a success, or a failure, we have begun to understand that the nature of who we are is love. God is spirit and God is love. Without our spirit we are nothing. Our spirit is who we are. We can choose.

Bill

During the time between those regular blood work tests and the hepatitis C tests, I thought I would wait for the proof before saying something. I knew that this was not the definition of faith. Faith is belief in things without evidence of the unseen. So I nervously told Pat Hannigan, a dear friend in our prayer group. We rejoiced together, believing in faith without having the results of the hepatitis C tests yet.

Then came the time for the hepatitis C test and nervously we had it done. I'll never forget it. Dr. Saris called me and said, "I don't know what to say. It looks like his liver decided to heal itself." I said, "Well, Dr. Saris, I've got to tell you something." I told her about the oil. She said, "Honey, I'd hold on to that if I were you."

I was so excited I could not wait to tell everyone. I even wrote a "special edition" of my annual letter and sent it out. They continued to monitor Stan's liver and blood tests and periodically do the hepatitis C test. In time, Dr. Saris referred us to Dr. Jeffrey Berman, who had joined the practice and specialized in hepatitis C. We saw him a couple of times, during which time testing for hepatitis C had greatly improved. There still was not a trace of it in Stan's test results. Dr. Berman questioned whether Stan ever had it and thought that maybe he was misdiagnosed. I sent him a copy of the biopsy. He didn't need to see Stan anymore, but suggested when Stan does his annual blood work that he include a hepatitis C test as well. The results have always been clean of hepatitis C since then.

After several years as an outpatient with Bryn Mawr, Stan was discharged. He has continued to see Dr. Long, however. After thoroughly researching several rehab programs, we started working with Main Line Rehab Associates. We have remained with them over the years. Several of the therapists we admired for their quality work were working at Main Line. A home therapy program was set up: speech, psychology, cognitive, job coaching, community integration, gym activities, and all sorts of tasks for functional living aimed at greater independence. There was an opportunity for Stan to assist with volunteer work at a nursing home in Neshaminy.

We changed funding programs over the years. With the help of family members, we have seen several rehab facilitators that we naturally compare to Bryn Mawr. They all fell short and didn't begin to compare.

In 1981, we built a home on Lake Wallenpaupack which we have had for twenty-two years. After Stan's crash, we severely cut back on having guests there, as I needed it for rest and relaxation. When we would boat, all the cares and tensions would fly away with the wind. As Stan became more active, and when he was in for his liver biopsy, Dr. Pagnanelli ordered an X-ray to see if he needed a plate put in his head to cover his deficit. He said he never expected Stan to be active so he didn't think of it. The X-ray showed that the muscles had covered the deficit well enough to protect him. The doctor preferred not to put a plate in so that the muscle would act like a window for the shunt. The shunt is just a mechanical device that needs to be replaced sometimes or swelling may occur in the brain. If it stops working correctly, we can see a bulge and try to manually pump it to determine if it needs to be replaced. Thank God for the muscle protection.

Doc asked Dr. Pagnanelli if Stan could water-ski, since he was an excellent skier and loved to do it. He replied by saying that he didn't think it was a good idea, given all his injuries, especially the neck injury sustained prior to the crash on February 27, 1986. But, if it meant that much to Stan and it was a risk he was willing to take, he obviously couldn't stop him. I was a wreck about it. I am a "better safe than sorry" kind of person. I explained to Stan that it could kill him, paralyze him from the neck down, or he could lose his leg if he broke it again. I made all this very clear to Stan, but of course he still wanted to do it. It blew my mind!

7-2-89

We got him a water-skiing helmet, and to the cheers and tears of friends and family he was skiing again on Lake Wallenpaupack. He lost one ski getting out of the water so he slalomed. He actually looked better on one ski, so we gave him back his O'Brien ski and he got up without kicking.

WaterSki Magazine
April 1990

In May 1991, we led a campaign to raise awareness about head injuries. A thousand bagged lights on the curbs of the streets lit the Meetinghouse Village section of Horsham, Pennsylvania.

Doc, Stan, and Louise

Bagged Lights

Some therapists had suggested in years past that we look into group homes for Stan. There, he might be put in situations that forced him to do activities. I collected information and tried to be objective, although he seemed as happy as a pig in %&$# at home. I took Stan to visit a friend and former Bryn Mawr patient who was living in a group home. We took him some toys to give to his son for Christmas. It seemed sad, as he was lying around, alone. Stan is a people person, and he might just sit in front of the TV or stay in his room in a place like that. I remember when Bryn Mawr had socials which Stan went to. I observed the people who attended from the group homes. I realized they have their place to help, but are only as good as the administration and staff who run them. I spoke with therapists as well. In the end, we made the decision to have Stan at home.

While Stan was going to Bryn Mawr as an outpatient, his speech therapist, Donna, told us about a program they were putting together. Bryn Mawr brain injury patients were going to talk to students at schools. They asked Stan to be a part of it since his crash was the result of drinking and driving. The program was written up in a national newspaper, *USA Today,* and was on television. I have the presentations on video. The format? A therapist would give a talk about traumatic injury and state the statistics. Following that, some survivors would share their story and the effect of it on their young lives. Even the rowdy audiences would settle down and you could hear sniffling around the auditorium. In addition to high schools, Stan gave presentations to a group at the local naval air station, a Bucks County, Pennsylvania, group charged with DWI (driving while intoxicated), the Rotary Club, and an alternative school. All total, beginning in 1991 and on into the next century, Stan gave over twenty presentations in the tri-state area (Pennsylvania, New Jersey, and Delaware).

I never got through a single presentation without crying. Because of Stan's speech problems, the organizers had to do this differently. They would explain that his part had to be conducted like an interview since Stan had difficulty putting together his thoughts and words. I prepared simple picture sheets on paper that were his answers to the interview question-and-answer format.

Once, a teacher saw what he was using for the answers and asked if she could pass it around for the students to see. Sometimes he moved his lips, trying to form the words he wanted to say. It could take a while for him to answer, yet the harder it was and the longer it took, the more powerful the message. The audiences would agonize with him. As time passed, we stopped practicing before the talks, because if they went too smoothly they weren't as effective. The students seeing a peer like this really hit them between the eyes!

Note: the Cruisin' not Boozin' Program at Bryn Mawr Behavioral Rehabilitation began around the same time as when Stan was asked to become involved. Today the program is expanding beyond drinking and driving. It addresses other distractions people engage in while driving, such as texting and cell phone use.

Louise

Stan's Cruisin' not Boozin' Notes

Note: Make sure Stan speaks into the microphone. In the past, both Stan and therapist had a tendency to look at each other while speaking and the microphone did not pick up everything. Note, though, that Stan benefits from visual cues and will probably need look at the speech pathologist.

Our next speaker is Stan Travis. He sustained a traumatic brain injury fifteen years ago as a result of a motor vehicle accident in which he was the passenger. He was at the Bent Elbow with some friends having a few beers. After drinking the beers, they got into their cars to drive to Nino's Pizza. They had a contest to see who could get there first by using different routes. They were speeding, talking, and not paying attention to the road. Stan hadn't buckled up and the driver was over the legal blood alcohol limit: a dangerous combination.

The driver lost control of his truck on the curve of the Willow Grove Turnpike exit ramp. The truck flipped lengthwise at least eight times uphill. Stan, who was not wearing his seat belt, was thrown from the truck.

We will conduct Stan's portion as an interview because he continues to have difficulty with starting speech, organizing what he wants to say, reading, and remembering. We appreciate your patience and silence. Distractions can make this more difficult for Stan. (This is effective.)

Question 1:   Tell us what injuries you received in the accident.

Stan: (He has picture cards for his answers but may need cueing.) 1. I died twice. 2. Fractured my skull from the top of my face through my cheek, face, eyes, and destroyed my sinuses. 3. Blind in left eye and tunnel vision only in my right. 4. Three operations on my brain; they took out part of my brain. 5. Could not talk. 6. Lost entire right side. 7. Got eighteen units of blood which gave me hepatitis C and liver damage. 8. Was in a coma for two months. 9. Ran a high temperature for weeks. 10. Wound up with grand mal seizures and can't drive my Corvette.

Question 2:   What was your life like before the accident?

Stan: Twenty-two years old, engaged, owned a two-year-old Corvette, fastest checker at Acme, and a service advisor at a Cadillac dealership.

Question 3:   What couldn't you do on your own that your therapist helped you with, and which are you still working on?

Stan: I couldn't walk, talk, use my right side, do math, read, write shower, shave, brush my teeth, or think.

Question 4:   How long were you hospitalized?

Stan: Three months in the hospital and five and a half months in Bryn Mawr.

Question 5:   How long has it been since your accident?

Stan: Fifteen years.

Question 6:   How did the accident affect your family and friends? (He may need help getting this part out.)

Stan: My brothers can't handle it. My mom sleeps in my room. I lost my independence, my friends, and my fiancée. My group of friends is broken.

Question 7A: How long has it been since you've gone out on a date?

Stan: Fourteen years.

Question 7B: Why are you giving this talk today?

Stan: To stop you, you, you, and you (he points to the audience).

Therapist: Many months after Stan's injury he was involved in another car accident. However, there were two important differences. Both Stan and his aide were wearing seat belts and neither was drunk. The vehicle rolled and landed on its roof, but both walked away from the accident.

New: Additional Questions

Therapist: After almost fourteen years since the accident, you were hospitalized in the Thomas Jefferson Hospital Neuro Intensive Care Unit (NICU) for one week. Why?

Stan: Seizures, seizures, seizures, seizures; hundreds of them.

Therapist: I understand that they had to give you so much medication to try to stop them that they were afraid of overdosing you. Then, after six medication changes, they finally stopped them. But now your liver has to be watched because of it. Do they know what brought them on?

Stan: No.

Last Question: What message would you like to leave with the audience?

Stan: Don't drink and drive, and buckle up.

Therapist: Thanks, Stan. As you can see, Stan has made a lot of progress, but speaking and thinking continue to be a challenge for him.

Note to therapist: If you take questions from the audience he'll have trouble. His mom will field them if he can't.

Original typed notes from some of Stan's talks

Louise

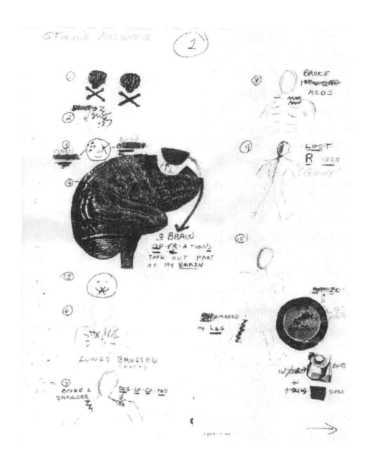

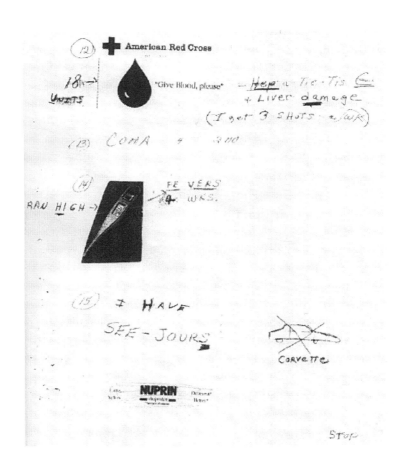

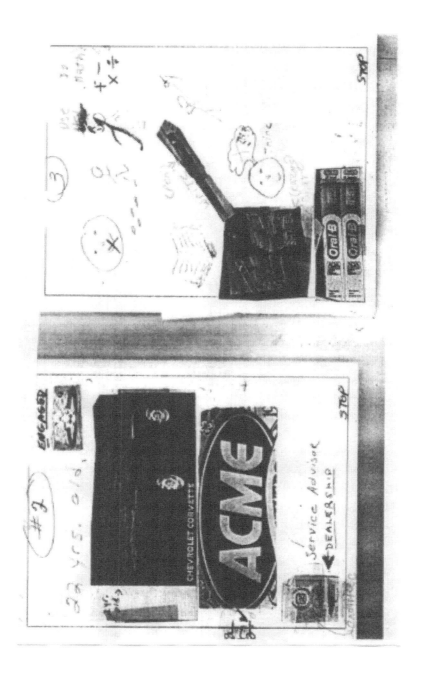

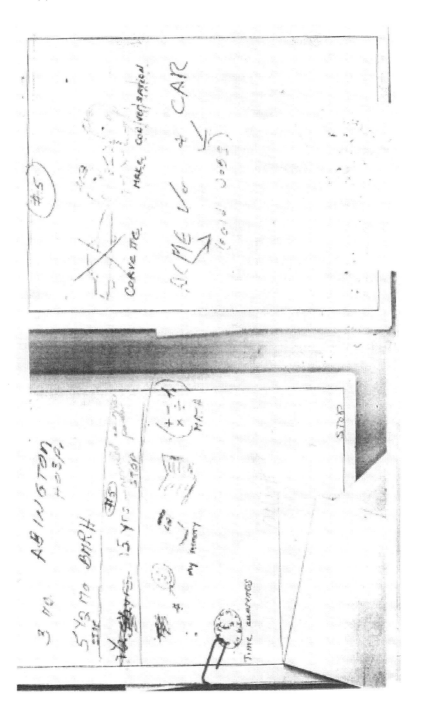

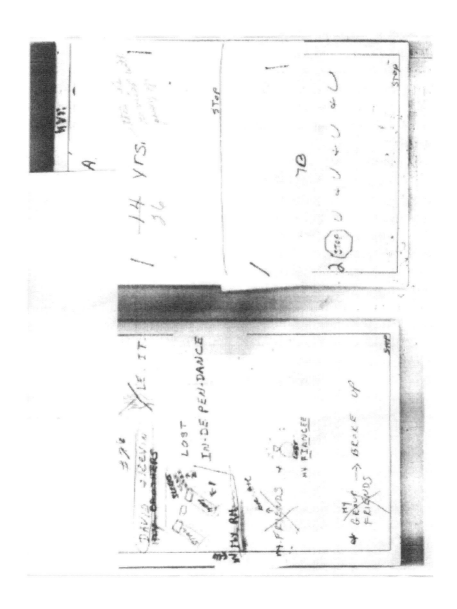

We don't condemn our wounded when they make mistakes. We welcome them back to life and walk with them.

Bill

1992

While in Bryn Mawr, they sent Stan to a local gym instead of traditional physical therapy. The program was called Fighting Back. The director of the program, Scott Dillman, and the people in this program worked with Stan one-on-one. Their efforts eliminated his limp when he walked and taught him to use a small gait instead, equalized his strength in both arms, and helped with his shoulder strength. Fighting Back had an awards night and Stan received an award for exemplifying the Fighting Back spirit.

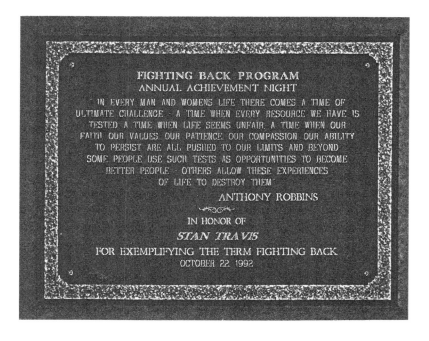

Fighting Back Program

Stan continued there until his funding ran out. Acme used to cover it as a union benefit, but those and other benefits were lost in later contracts for part-time employees. Fighting Back has an annual awards night and fund-raiser for scholarships for those that are not covered by insurance. When Stan threw his 300 game, they recognized it, gave a talk about him, and showed the video of the game. The applause was thunderous and moving!

1996

After taking up bowling years before and having bowled with his dad in a league, Stan was beginning to find success and recognition with bowling. He bowled in different leagues and in 1996 his team won trophies for their performance. He also received an American Bowling Congress (ABC) special recognition medal honoring his many accomplishments since 1986. He has received other medals and awards as well. For example, one was for the most improved average and another for the number of games over two hundred. The mixed (men and women) league, the men's bowling league, and the gym all offer Stan social time with peers in a real-world setting instead of rehab. Stan seems to enjoy people of all ages — infants to the elderly.

2000

We all went to Disney World to celebrate the new millennium with family and friends. Sixty-five to seventy people spanning four generations were present.

First trip back to Disney World
Left to right: Uncle Norman Cataldi, Dad, Mom, Stan

The body, mind, and spirit are connected. For some reason, Stan began having major seizure activity in February 2000, around the crash anniversary date. He started with migraines, heavy breathing patterns, and feeling anxious. Then…

2-7-00

12:45 a.m. Stan stated, "Something is going to happen!" Then he had a full-blown seizure. He reported feeling hyper, shaking inside, tapping both legs; he was weak, numb, and felt a tingling sensation. His breaths per minute were thirty-five (normal BPM is fourteen). Louise gave him extra seizure medication.

1:25 a.m. Stan called "Mom!" and began shaking violently from head to toe. He was aware and feeling scared. His face was twisted, he couldn't feel or move his right leg, and his BPM was thirty-seven. He reported having a major headache, his heart rate (HR) was eighty-six, and his right hand was cold. Doc advised to administer one more phenobarbital. Stan had two more seizures after that. Louise cried out for Doc, but he was very sick that night. She handled it herself.

3:02 a.m. Another seizure arrived, lasting fifteen to twenty seconds. Louise gave him another phenobarbital. He could move his right arm but not his leg.

4:56 a.m. Stan had another one. He went to the bathroom after each one when he felt he could make it there with assistance. Louise would take one of his arms and wrap it around her neck and shoulders, hold it with one, and use the other to support his weight with it wrapped around his body.

5:11 a.m. Headache pain was still really bad and not subsiding. Louise called Bryn Mawr and was told to get him to the ER. Louise called Main Line Rehab and left a message on their machine, telling them what was happening and to cancel his job coach for the day. She called Acme to inform them that he would not be to work that day. She got dressed, dressed Stan, and left Doc a note. At the ER, they hooked Stan up to some monitors and did a CT scan, an X-ray, and blood work. He had had another one around 7:05 a.m. Phenobarbital level was forty-six and the CT was unchanged since the last two. The neurologist discussed several things, ruled out various causes, and couldn't figure out why this was happening. He said he would consult with Dr. Long.

12:55 p.m.
Louise and Stan returned home. She took care of Doc, as he was still feeling pretty ill. While Stan was in the recliner waiting for Louise he had another seizure which lasted about thirty seconds.

1:17 p.m.
Louise and Stan ate lunch and took a nap around 3:00 p.m. His right leg still was not operational.

4:25 p.m.

Stan had another big seizure lasting about thirty seconds. Louise gave him another phenobarbital. Doc said to also begin administering the Neurontin which was prescribed at the ER. Before going to bed, Louise gave Stan another Neurontin and waited for it to kick in before going to sleep.

2-8-00

Louise spoke to Dr. Long in the afternoon, got medication instructions, and was told to call back in a couple days or sooner if needed. The seizure activity continued all week. There were so many that she kept a stroke count instead of the normal entries to the seizure log.

While at the hospital for some tests later that week, he had three very close together: at the registration desk, in the EEG reception area, and during his tests. The hospital staff was amazed that Stan remembered them. He continues to be anxious and fearful. Because the seizures numbered so many, Louise began using a tape recorder to chart them. All this continued to happen in spite of increasing the meds.

Louise

Stan's seizure condition continued like this throughout most of February 2000. The neighbors helped them out. Stan was admitted to the Thomas Jefferson Hospital Epilepsy Unit in Philadelphia on February 12, 2000. Sue Ann Butts's six-foot-five-inch husband, Richard, came over and got Stan down the steps, put him on a desk chair with wheels, and rolled him to the car. Stan had two seizures in the car, one while waiting for his room at the hospital, and many more throughout the night. While on her way to the room with Stan, Louise sidestepped two policemen escorting a handcuffed man down the hallway. She stayed with Stan that night.

No matter how much medication was given, the seizures continued at this alarming rate. After making some twenty-five phone calls, the cardiology nursing supervisor got Stan a place in the Neurology Intensive Care Unit (NICU). Louise began recording all Stan's seizures since the staff was busy and did not. She was not allowed to stay overnight, but was allowed an early arrival on Monday to assist with feeding Stan and to continue helping with him. There were long periods of time when Stan was alone with his seizure activity in the NICU.

Louise traveled on the train down to Jefferson Monday morning. She noticed that the conductor knew most of the passengers as regulars and made some nice comments to everyone in the car: "Happy Valentine's Day." Louise fought off her emotions welling up inside. She arrived at 11:15 a.m. to find Stan sad, depressed, and spacing. Louise felt the same way she had at AMH fourteen years earlier. Her heart sank when she looked at her son. Then she said, "Don't you give up on me!" It was difficult for him to lift his spirits, but with time he did it.

Louise was introduced to a neurosurgeon in his room. Her heart missed a beat. The plan was to get Stan to the Epilepsy Care Unit (ECU) where they could have him monitored on TV, microphone, and computer. Louise would stay the rest of the week and continue her seizure log. On February 15, Stan's godmother and Louise's sister, Helen, and her husband, Emil, came to see Stan. The doctors were frequently outside Stan's room. Louise observed the head nurse pacing in the room. The nurse commented, "There's a fine line between efforts to stop the seizures and overdosing him. Decisions may have to be made. He is not stable and may have to go back to NICU."

Louise called Doc to update him. She suggested that the boys drive him down. Any decisions about another brain surgery or anything else were too important for her to make alone, she thought. Doc stayed overnight, too, and they took turns sleeping in the lounge. They continued to monitor Stan's seizure activity. Each time he had one he would press the button. They would note the time and what effect it had on his body.

In the morning, the nurses and Louise changed Stan's bed, bathed him, and family and friends began to arrive. Doc spoke with Dr. Sperling when he came around. They agreed that the medication being used was like pouring water into Stan with no effect. They decided to try Dilantin and monitor his liver functions daily. Stan's last seizure was at 10:45 a.m. on February 16, 2000. Dr. Sperling and his associates were on top of the situation. The EEG technician, who was staying after his shift had ended, came in and flashed Louise a great big smile, saying, "He really had us scared."

More visitors came to visit Stan the next few days. Dr. Sperling came in and asked Stan to walk. He wanted Stan up, out of bed, walking, sitting in the chair, walking in his room and in the hall with assistance, and going to the recreation room that night. He ordered a physical therapy (PT) evaluation for the next day. Stan's liver functions had been okay and dermatology said his rash was not medication-related. To combat the nosebleeds and a sore elbow, a vaporizer and ibuprofen, respectively, were ordered. It took Stan some time to get the functioning of his right leg back.

The PT evaluation suggested seven to ten days of inpatient rehabilitation. After Dr. Sperling checked him, he concluded the tiredness and effect of the meds would pass, and that discharge could be Saturday, February 19. They kept Stan out of bed a lot on Friday and that night. He was in the recreation room with other patients and the nurses' aides, watching videos and playing cards.

Saturday arrived and so did the discharge instructions. They got Stan showered, dressed, and packed. Anne picked them up from the hospital and they stopped by to visit with family on the way. There was lots of company at the house. Stan tried to nap and Anne stayed with him while Louise went to mass.

After they returned home, Stan was walking well at times but unstable at other times. He was more confused and showed more short-term memory loss now than prior to February 2000. His motivation and initiative were lower, and he was a bit more resistant and stubborn. The alien leg syndrome had returned as well. Stan's blood work was good. The PT came to the house, did an evaluation, and gave Stan exercises to do. His right side was weaker and he was unsteady and wobbled at times. He'd take a few steps, sidestep, take a step back, and then continue walking.

He surprised himself by this sometimes and didn't always seem to understand what was being said.

Stan turned forty in 2003. All he wanted for a gift was a party with his family. When he went to see Dr. Sperling for his regular checkup, the doctor said, "I hate to tell you, but it is all down-hill from here." At first Louise thought he was joking, as many people often do when someone turns forty. Then it occurred to her that he was not one to joke around. He said Stan's cognitive, motor, and balance skills would begin to slip. They started addressing his fine motor skills with his therapists and worked with the gym to address his balance issues.

While an outpatient at Bryn Mawr, Stan was in a car accident with his driver aide. The car was run off the road, went up an embankment, and rolled over. Stan and the driver both had their seat belts on and were hanging upside down. Louise got a call from Paoli Hospital that they were okay. She spoke with both the driver and Stan. As a result of that incident, Stan now carries with him a medical alert card and other pertinent information about his condition.

One Sunday at mass, Louise passed a dear friend of hers, Jeanette McDermott, and they acknowledged each other while on their way up to receive communion. Jeanette's mother asked who Louise was. She explained to her mother that Louise was the mother who wouldn't let her son die. Louise was a bit uncomfortable and embarrassed about that. While up in the mountains some time later, Louise was about to pick up a magazine and for some reason thought she'd read from the Bible instead. She opened directly to a passage which read: "Some women through faith, received their loved ones back from the dead."

In 2005, Stan was experiencing stomach pains which persisted. Tests concluded that it was his gall bladder. It was removed.

There are no coincidences. What we think about and act upon shows up in our life. When we believe something with all our heart and mind, and act, *It*'ll show up. That's how *It* works. Keep the faith. We attract *It*.

As the years passed, they began to forget about the February 1986 anniversary date. More healing was taking place.

300
January 25, 2011

Dad was the first Stan wanted to tell. Then, he went to see Uncle Norman and Aunt Mary, Grandmom Travis, and Aunt Anne. Then, they called his brothers, Dave and Kevin, and Aunt Helen and Uncle Emil. It was time to stop for the night, but there were many more calls the next day — incoming and outgoing. They went through two batteries on the cordless. The excitement level was at an all-time high! That next day, Doc's secretary called the newspaper, the *Intelligencer*. Doc was eventually put in touch with reporter Phil Gianficaro; he gave him some information and then referred him to Louise for more details. Pictures were taken at the Lanes. Stan's brothers were so excited and they posted the news on Facebook. The man in charge of the pro shop at Thunderbird Lanes in Warminster, Gus Claeys, got Stan a bowling pin; painted on it were his name, 300, and the date. The bowling league president, Kathy Kelly, spoke with Louise. She said that another good bowler and a real nice person, John Strobel, had bowled a 300 game in another league that was sanctioned by the American Bowling Congress (ABC). Stan's league was not. John wanted Stan's ring size, intending to give Stan his ring, which he hadn't ordered yet.

Sunday was the day the piece would run in the *Intelligencer*. Doc woke early and went to 7-Eleven for copies.

The story was the headline — front page and in color! Doc was cooked up and brimming with excitement. He rushed around the house and woke everyone up. They read it to Stan with tear-filled eyes and a lump in the throat. The Travises celebrated Grandmom Travis's ninety-sixth birthday. Aunt Anne had put Stan's picture and 300 game on one half of the cake and Grandmom Travis's picture on the other half. Stan was presented with the 300 pin, and all the partygoers received a copy of the newspaper.

The cards, gifts, and phone calls continued rolling in. The parish priest called and left a message that was filled with excitement. Dr. Anne Saris called and left a message for Stan also. She was so excited for him! Louise made an audio cassette tape for Stan with all the congratulatory phone messages. She also made a scrapbook and a mix of fifteen songs that have been special for Stan as he has been connecting the dots back to perfection.

Stan's Mix

Song	Artist	Meaning
"One Moment in Time"	Whitney Houston	
"Celebration"	Kool and the Gang	
"I'm So Excited"	The Pointer Sisters	
"So Emotional"	Whitney Houston	
"The Impossible Dream"	*Man of La Mancha* soundtrack	Rehabilitation
"How Great Are You Lord"	Robin Mark/*Revival in Belfast*	Bowling 300
"I'm Comin' Out So You Better Get This Party Started"	No Doubt	What God has been for the Travises
"We Are Family"	Sister Sledge	
"I'll Be There for You"	Bon Jovi	Louise's promise to Stan
"Because You Loved Me"	Celine Dion	Stan III and Louise's song
"That's What Friends Are For"	Dionne Warwick and Friends	Friends during the hospital
"Livin' on a Prayer"	Bon Jovi	What we're doing and are continuing
"Nothing's Gonna Stop Us Now"	Jefferson Starship	Pure motivation
"Hero"	Mariah Carey	What Stan is
"How Great Thou Art"	Elvis Presley	What God has done

Doc got a call from Lisa Santoro, a CBS-TV show network producer who had seen the newspaper article. Doc thought the caller said CVS, as in CVS Pharmacy. Once CBS was made clear, Doc handed off the call to Louise.

Louise and Doc got a couple of cakes, one which they ate and two which they took to Thunderbird Lanes for a party. The Travises hosted parties on back-to-back nights, with plenty of copies of the article, plus cake and refreshments. On February 9, 2011, Bill Little, the general manager of Thunderbird Lanes, opened early for the CBS-TV show cameraman, Erick Regan, to get ready for the interview broadcast.

The night Stan was presented with the 300 ring, every league bowling in the building at Thunderbird Lanes stopped and the presentation was done over the public address system.

Stan's fellow league bowler, Theresa Gibson, shot video the night Stan bowled his 300. The last couple frames were posted on YouTube: Stan Travis bowls. Dave and Kevin made it available to everyone. Kevin called his mom one morning and read to her what people were writing in response to Stan's 300. It was mind-blowing. People want to hear good news! There were responses from all over the USA and around the world! After Kevin finished reading it to his mom, Louise asked him to read it to Stan and Dad. Kevin responded, "Are you kidding me? I had a hard enough time getting this out to you!"

"More healing has begun," Louise said to herself after hanging up the phone with her son. Louise and Doc's grandson was passing it on where he went to music school in Boston. Everyone was healing. So much had been pushed inside for so long, Louise thought. Stan was doing something really, really big. This was big for anyone, and Stan was doing it! More healing for everyone.

For almost a year people everywhere continued to congratulate Stan. In a department store one day, a woman passed Stan, stopped, and then said, "Hey, aren't you the person, the bowler I saw in the newspaper?" Louise sent copies of the article to Stan's medical team and to the hospitals and rehabs to post and give hope to people. Bryn Mawr Rehab took Stan's photo while he was at an appointment with Dr. Long.

On March 28, 2011, Scott Dillman, the director of the Fighting Back program, called. Stan was going to be recognized at their annual awards night, and would be present with Scott as the newest program members were being recognized. Acme took Stan's picture and his story was highlighted in its newsletter.

Congratulations to Stan Travis at the New Britain store! Thanks, Stan, for all you do for the company, customers, and associates!

Acme Newsletter, May 2011

Stan attended his thirtieth high school reunion in the fall of 2011. Many came up and congratulated him. Some were buddies he bowled with in high school, and one was a guy he played basketball with in elementary school. This guy still has the article from the *Hatboro Horsham Alumni News* on his desk, which was titled:

After years of adversity, a night of perfection.

On January 25, 2011, Stan fell in the first game, scoring a 164. He rebounded in the second game to bowl a 195, and then finished it off with his 300.

On March 6, 2012, Stan threw six strikes, a (9/-) spare, and finished with five more strikes for a 279 game—eleven strikes and one spare. Stan threw a 665 series in May 2012.

Thunderbird Lanes - Warminster

1475 W. Street Road - WARMINSTER

(215)674-8250

1/25/2011					Score by player						8:47:16PM

STAN TRAVIS	1	2	3	4	5	6	7	8	9	10	Total
Lane 14			Game 1				1/25/2011 18.33			19.14	
Hdcp 0	8 /	8 1	9 /	⑦ 1	X	X	X	7 2	6 3	X 7 1	
	18	27	44	52	82	109	128	137	146	164	**164**
Lane 14			Game 2				1/25/2011 19.17			19.59	
Hdcp 0	X	X	X	7 /	7 1	9 /	X	X	9 /	6 2	
	30	57	77	94	102	122	151	171	187	195	**195**
Lane 14			Game 3				1/25/2011 20.02			20.46	
Hdcp 0	X	X	X	X	X	X	X	X	X	X X X	
	30	60	90	120	150	180	210	240	270	300	**300**

Thunderbird Lanes - Warminster

1475 W. Street Road - WARMINSTER

(215)674-8250

3/6/2012					Score by player						8:23:00PM

STAN TRAVIS	1	2	3	4	5	6	7	8	9	10	Total
Lane 13			Game 1				3/6/2012 18.38			19.31	
Hdcp 0	X	X	X	9 /	X	7 /	X	X	9 /	8 1	
	30	59	79	99	119	139	168	188	206	215	**215**
Lane 13			Game 2				3/6/2012 19.32			20.18	
Hdcp 0	X	X	X	X	X	X	9 /	X	X	X X X	
	30	60	90	120	149	169	189	219	249	279	**279**

Thunderbird Lanes - Warminster

1475 W. Street Road - WARMINSTER

(215)674-8250

Score by player

lanes 11 12
5/15/2012 bowled
5/16/2012 *print out*

point out - 11:48:38AM

STAN TRAVIS		1	2	3	4	5	6	7	8	9	10	Total
Lane 11				Game 1				5/15/2012 18.41			19.24	
Hdcp	0	8 /	X	8 /	7 /	8 1	X	X	X	X	X X 8	
		20	40	57	75	84	114	144	174	204	232	232
Lane 11				Game 2				5/15/2012 19.28			20.11	
Hdcp	0	5 4	X	9 /	X	X	X	X	8 /	8 -	X X 9	
		9	29	49	79	109	137	157	175	183	212	212
Lane 11				Game 3				5/15/2012 20.15			21.13	
Hdcp	0	X	X	⑦ 2	X	X	X	X	9 /	⑨ 1	X X x	
		27	46	55	85	115	144	164	182	191	221	221

665 Total

League president Kathy Kelly presenting Stan with his 300 ring

300 Game Party
Left to right: Doc, David, Stan, Louise, Kevin

Stan and his brother Dave admiring the ring

Ninety-six-year-old Grandmom Sara Travis and Stan

Stan gets a hug from his nephew

John Strobel and Stan

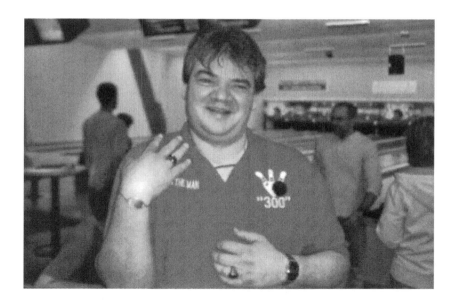

Stan

Chet Shehoski and Stan holding a trophy Chet made for him

The Intelligencer article and photos hanging on the wall
at Thunderbird Lanes in Warminster, Pennsylvania

CHAPTER SEVEN

LOVE AND SUPPORT -
SOME OF STAN'S TEAM

Brother and Doctor
My profession is a cardiologist.
I chose this profession because my father was a physician and it always seemed like what I was supposed to do. I always thought that I would be a family doc, but I found that a bit boring and found cardiology so easy that it seemed like a natural fit. Being a cardiologist is interesting. I love helping people, especially at times when they are most in need. What I like most about the profession is to bring something to it that a lot of physicians don't. I am not a typical doc in any way. I am an artist, a hunter, a landscaper, and a dad. I love to photograph things. I love to work out and am passionate about it. I used to smoke, and love that I did. I love speaking freely about how hard it is to quit. In short, I really like to surprise people and be very open with them. I like being friends with my patients. Being with someone when they die, when the veil between the worlds is at its thinnest,

is one of the most blessed things I have ever experienced. Over the years, I have learned to appreciate time—time with friends, family, patients, and alone. The balance is the hard part.

My best day of work is one where I help people, have fun doing it, and don't feel like I am going crazy doing so.

The worst day is when all I get out of the entire day is work. I hate days like that.

It's still very hard for me to speak about Stan. When I first saw him after the accident:

He was my brother.

He was my best friend.

He was almost dead.

He should have been dead.

We were told he was dying. He got last rites. He was going to be an organ donor.

It was a mess.

The Stan that I knew did die in that accident, as did the family I knew and the self that I knew.

This is really too much for me to write. It's a story with so many paths, so many obstacles, so much sorrow, resentment, and then acceptance…sort of.

I'm happy that Stan's life has been mostly joyful.

I'm very happy that he has no real pain physically or emotionally.

I wish he had more, but he seems content, which is such a blessing. He may be more content than me sometimes. I keep wishing for more for him. Some sort of miracle where one day, he could just talk without hesitation, walk without hesitation, and live without hesitation.

I really would love just one more day with the Stan of my youth. Makes me feel greedy, but it's the truth.

The God in this life thing is difficult for me. The unfairness of it all is still hard to grasp.

The 300 game? Gave us all hope. It made me believe again. There is really no other explanation for it than Divine Intervention. I have the article from the paper in one of my exam rooms and my patients read it all the time. This is what I tell them:

There is just no reason that a nearly blind man who cannot really walk ten feet without stumbling should be able to throw a 300 game unless God was at his side. Just no other way! That game brought more healing to me and my family than all the other days leading up to it combined. Stan had a moment in the sun in the middle of a life where none of us would have imagined it possible. It still makes me cry.

Thanks, Bill, for doing this. It means so much to my mom, maybe even more than to Stan, and Mom deserves as much joy as can be sent her way. Her smile was bright as a young woman's, and any way to see it again is so welcome.

Love and peace to you, now and in all you do.

Dr. David Travis

An Ophthalmologist

I chose this profession as I always wanted to be a physician since childhood. I was always fascinated by science and chemistry and how things work. I specifically chose ophthalmology in my senior year of medical school. I had a choice of several rotations and I listed ophthalmology as one of the choices. I had no exposure to ophthalmology in the past. I had healthy eyes and everyone in my family had healthy eyes. Once I did this rotation, I was fascinated by the visual system. I have always liked cameras and photography, and obviously the eye functions very similar to a camera. I was just fascinated by the different equipment we could use to examine the eye. With some of this equipment, we could even see individual cells flowing through the blood vessels. I can honestly say that the eye is the window to the body. There are many diseases we can diagnose with the eye. So, I liked the fact that usually we can find an answer to a person's problem through our careful examination of the eyes and the visual system.

Now that I have practiced ophthalmology for quite a few years, I think what I enjoy most is the ability it gives me to help people and to impact people's lives in a positive way. The most obvious way I can impact them is through things like cataract surgery, when I can physically remove the cloudy human cataract and replace it with a clear lens. It is very rewarding to be able to help patients see better. It is also rewarding to help people preserve their vision. There are some patients, of course, that I cannot help, and these patients are a challenge for me to try to help them cope with their disability. I try to point out the positives and what they do have, and not what they don't have. I would say that working with Stan has helped me so much in this particular area. He has helped me focus on the positive rather than the negative with my patients. In fact, I sometimes use him as an example to patients, to show them just how much can be done with some limitation to one's sight.

My profession also gives me the opportunity to try to help people cope with their losses in other areas. I often see patients every six months or one year, depending on the health of their eyes or if they have any eye disease. Very often, I will have a husband and wife come in together for these appointments for ten to fifteen years. And, then I will have a visit where the patient comes in alone or with a son or daughter, and this usually means that the spouse has passed away or has been institutionalized. These are always particularly sad visits. I often leave the room with tears in my eyes. However, I always try to give words of encouragement in these situations, to try to help get them through the exam, that day, and that week.

I am a fairly religious person and have gotten more so over the years. Before I operate, I always pray to God that he will work through me to help these patients. People are often very thankful after their cataract surgery. I always try to deflect the thanks to God above. Sometimes I just point up to the heavens, and sometimes I will say things to the patient. Some people will say, "Thank you so much for all you have done" and "Thank God everything came out right." I always tell them to reverse the order; obviously, thankfulness needs to go to God. I feel in my life, both personally and professionally, I have been very blessed. He has made me more spiritual. Why have I been so blessed and others not? I always try to be very thankful for my blessings and, by the same token, try to help others as I can.

My best day practicing is when all my patients are doing well. This is when their eye pressures are low, they are seeing well from the cataract surgery, and everyone is pretty satisfied. My worst days are when I have complicated cataract surgery that doesn't go quite the way I wanted it to. I am always thinking there is something I could have done differently to have prevented it. It is hard to feel that I could have done more or done something differently to help prevent a complication. Fortunately, thank God, most of these patients do well even with the complications.

I began practicing in the Hatboro, Pennsylvania, area in the mid-1980s, close to where Stan Sr. (Doc) practices. I shared a lot of patients with Doc and we certainly knew of each other. Doc is incredibly dedicated to his patients. He is more of the old-style family doc where he works independently. He is the type of physician that makes himself available to his patients 24/7. I have always respected Doc for this and knew that he was loved by his patients.

I remember vividly first seeing Stan. Obviously, he was involved in this very tragic auto accident with his teenage friend, and was in the neuro intensive care unit at Abington Memorial Hospital. He had multiple facial trauma and a brain hemorrhage, and I was consulted to try to evaluate his vision. I remember when I went to see Stan. I think I was seeing him for the second time. Doc was there and was distraught. Stan had increased intracranial pressure from the brain hemorrhage. The increase in intracranial pressure actually exerted a lot of downward force on the brain in what we call a brain herniation. This is a tragic consequence and can often lead to death. I walked in on this situation. Doc had tears in his eyes and was distraught, but yet still extended a kind greeting to me. Stan was intubated at this time, of course, and was nonresponsive, from the brain hemorrhage, the brain swelling and herniation, as well as medication. It was impossible to evaluate his vision. I could only examine the structure of the globes themselves, which did appear intact. My thoughts at this point were that this was a tragedy and my heart went out to the parents. I was helpless in this situation, as the main issue was the brain injuries and not the eyeball injuries. I now realize that as I have matured in my profession, I could have and should have offered more comfort.

At that point it was not clear at all if Stan Jr. would even survive his massive brain injuries and secondary herniation. I certainly couldn't begin to anticipate what kind of visual function he might have. Stan then went through a nearly miraculous recovery. I probably next saw him three, four, or six months after this episode, when he had recovered so much of his neurologic function. At this time, many months later, I was able to assess Stan's visual function. What we found was that Stan had essentially one-quarter of his vision in one eye only. I believe he can only see out of the left upper quadrant of his left eye. He lost the right half of his vision in both eyes from the original brain hemorrhage. I believe, then, that when the brain herniated, the right optic nerve was affected, and he became totally blind in the right eye and lost the inferior half of his vision in his left eye.

I have followed Stan from that time to the present on a yearly basis. Sharing Stan's progress and development has been a great pleasure. The total unmitigated love, support, and encouragement given to Stan by his parents have been a wonderful phenomenon to behold. Mrs. Travis (Louise) has included me in their Christmas cards and it has made me feel a part of their extended family. I feel so fortunate to have been included in a very tiny part of this amazing story. Mrs. Travis once sent me a small article she ran across about comparing her life to a trip where they thought they were going to Italy but ended up in some other country. The point was that although their life was not what they had planned, where they ended up was every bit as beautiful and as meaningful and as full as it possibly could have been. I recall sharing this piece with one of my friends who had the misfortune of having a child with autism. I know he was thankful for the piece and it was inspiring to him.

One amazing part of this whole story is Stan's 300 game of bowling. I think I perhaps became aware of it through newspaper articles, but it was an absolutely wonderful experience for

Stan to accomplish this goal that is so rare. Any bowler would be so proud of such a feat. To accomplish this feat with one-quarter vision in one eye is almost beyond belief. I know I had tears in my eyes the day I learned about this, and also the next visit I had with Stan in the office with his mom, when we shared and relived that experience together.

I feel so privileged and enriched to have known Stan and his mom and dad throughout the past twenty-five years. It is a story of the power of love, support, prayer, and faith. It is the story of the triumph of the human spirit. It is the story of taking what we are given or what we have and making the absolute most of it, not the least. It is a story that I sometimes use with my patients that are sorrowful over the loss of a part of their vision. I can always bring up the story of Stan Travis and his 300 game! Stan has done more with one-quarter vision in one eye than so many of us do with full vision in both eyes. He and his family are an inspiration to us all.

Having seen Stan throughout these last twenty years, I have watched what a great personality he has. He always greets me with a smile and a handshake, and is happy to see me. He never fails to tell me what he has been up to and, despite the incredible brain injury which he has largely overcome, he always manages to brighten my day. I expect he brightens the days of the people who are lucky enough, like myself, to come in contact with him. I am one of the many fortunate people to know Stan Travis and his mom and dad.

Dr. Thomas A. Armstrong

Teacher, Neighbor, and Friend

Sue Ann Butts moved into the Horsham neighborhood in 1978 or 1979. Her son was seven years old and her daughter was eleven. It was a close-knit community.

"We lived directly behind the Travises. I get tears in my eyes when I think about how the Travises included us in everything. Our kids played volleyball and baseball together in the field between our houses. They invited us to use their pool whenever we wanted, and to join in their holiday picnics and parties which were twice each summer. I remember the adults sitting out all night during the summers while the children would play. Stan (born in 1963) would always make sure my son Tommy (born in 1971, and the youngest of the neighborhood kids) was part of the team, and would always take Tommy with the other kids to play."

Sue Ann went on to say what phenomenal people the Travises are and what a wonderful experience it was having them as neighbors.

"There was drinking involved in the crash and the laws were not as stringent then. Nor was the awareness and laws regarding seat belt use. I never get off the Willow Grove exit today without thinking of him. I remember going down to the hospital thinking, how would he survive?

"Louise, Doc, Stan, and the rest of the family handled this with a tremendous amount of faith. It sustains us. I think of Louise as an angel. I think it was frustrating for Doc to watch and not be able to do anything. Stan continues to be a wonderful part of their lives. Everyone continues to support each other. I think the crash pulled them closer together. It was interesting to watch Stan recognize his new limitations. I watched him play cards again. I would take him to bowling practice when Louise couldn't due to surgery on each of her knees. I remember being aware that he could have a seizure at any time and the responsibility that I had being with him. When driving him, I remember Stan giving me directions.

"My husband Dick died a few years ago. Toward the end of his life at home with me, Doc would always come over and check in on Dick. During Dick's final weeks, when the other doctors were pulling back their care, Doc filled the gaps. Once, he came over at 4:00 a.m. He has always been there."

Phone interview with Sue Ann Butts

Stan's Friend

I am a cabinetmaker. I come from a family of tradespeople and it was the only one not taken. I had always enjoyed building with Dad's scrap lumber. I have built wood objects and other things since I was in my early teens — toys, trucks, and even bridges across the creek. One year I found an abandoned horse corral. As you can imagine, I had lots of fun with that. I can spend a few hours, days, weeks, or months on a project, but when I'm done there is always something to look at. It's handmade. It's visual. I like that. My work has made me visualize everything. A strong artistic side of me is involved.

My career choice allows my schedule to be flexible. In 2008, I even got involved in yoga. In 2007, I was totally engulfed in my work. Yoga has slowed me down. I eat healthy and am more at peace. When I am done building something I take great pride in it — the quality, the workmanship — I visualize every step when I'm listening to what a customer is requesting. I instinctively and automatically calculate the expenses, the material, what I'm gonna have to do, the potential hazards, and so forth. As I've gotten older, though, I also now consider my work more of a way of income and providing for my family. I'm grateful. As I was beginning to grow my business, I was doing work only for contractors. This commercial work was more exact and more predictable.

Picture this. Where I work, the front (side-by-side doors) and the back (two large hinged garage doors) are open, with both a breeze and the sun's rays coming through. Through the doors I see a lot of trees. It's very scenic and I can see all of nature. This is my best day working. Nice! My worst day is when I built something and was moving too fast, hurrying, was distracted, and ended up needing to pull it apart and start again from scratch. I've gotten a lot better. Maybe it's the yoga!

After the crash, my first thoughts were, *Oh my God, I can't take this back. Things would change — forever.* Initially, Stan had a broken leg and a cut lip. Stan recognized everyone when he arrived at Abington Memorial Hospital. He gave the usual nod as if to say,

"Everything is okay, how are you?" He shook my hand, but at the same time had a look as if he was wondering what had just happened. When I saw Stan at Bryn Mawr Rehabilitation after his brain had swelled, it was really scary. He was in a scary state.

What surprised me the most, initially, was him walking again. And then, years later, bowling a perfect 300 game was huge! His forgiveness, also. But it's difficult to call it that. Part of me wishes he would remember it. His body movements and behavior and a lot of that are the old Stan, but I can't sit and talk with him like the old days.

His brother Dave introduced me and my wife. Recently, after Stan's mom and dad's fiftieth wedding anniversary celebration, I was looking at the all-American family from years back. To see it all laid out and how the family has changed was difficult for me. So many times Mrs. Travis (I have to call her Mrs. Travis and not "Weesie," out of the great respect I have for her) has gone out of her way to comfort me. "It's okay, stop worrying," she would say. It's like she just wants me to be okay with myself.

Stan and I went to school together. I realized I wanted a career in fine woodwork and not construction. Stan went automotive. There was their mountain home and we were two young kids in an apartment. We spent weekends and college together. We were quite normal.

I've changed myself over the years. I'm a little more comfortable, maybe, a little more outgoing. I used to be the quiet one of the group. As I've grown a little older, maybe I've become a little wiser. Recently I was working with my son on a project. He was on the ladder, drilling a hole at the top of the post. I was holding the ladder for him. I was silent as he was working. I was allowing him and trusting him that in the end he would be okay with what he was accomplishing. He's confident enough and I knew he could do it. He did a great job. I had let go of my need to have this job be perfect. It was a symbolic "passing of the torch." *I'm finally getting better*, I thought.

I grew up with the Catholic religion. Today, I'm not a very religious person, but I've come to believe in the power of prayer. The power of prayer — amazing! Weesie believes in the spirit and spiritual prayer. I believe in the science of prayer. I have learned about noetic science — to create weight with prayer that can lead to change. It's amazing!

Phone interview

Cousin and Friend

Hello!

A few words about Louise Travis come to mind.

Having known Louise as a cousin and as a friend from child-hood on through the golden years, I find her to be an absolutely amazing person. She is kind to everyone, regardless of age, appearance, intelligence, occupation, financial status, etc. She has a remarkable knack of spotting the one person in a crowd who doesn't feel quite as confident as he or she should and speaking to him or her in a way that changes all that. She is always think-ing of how something will impact other people. She loves to plan ahead and make things just right for everyone. She does all this in a very understated way, and rarely lets anyone know the time and effort involved.

I believe that Stan Travis would not have been able to recover to the point that he has if it had not been for Louise Travis. He is truly lucky to have her for a mother, and all of us are lucky to have her as a relative/friend.

Thank you for sharing their story!

Mrs. Theresa Scholly

Family Friend

My husband, Paul, and I count our blessings, but don't exam-ine how God is at work in our daily lives. That being said, we admire the tremendous faith of Doc and Louise, and acknowl-edge how it has sustained them over the years since Stan's crash. Although surrounded by a large circle of family and friends, I believe that their faith is the principal reason they have survived this long, ongoing journey with Stan.

It is about how God has played a part in Stan's and his family's healing that I can offer my thoughts. Perhaps the relationship we share with the Travis family has been the work of God? The relationship has been a blessing in many respects. Perhaps God brought Stan and Paul together for this reason?

Paul's relationship with Stan began in the summer of 1983, when he was introduced to Stan by his friend, the driver of the truck involved in the crash. Paul and Stan quickly became friends, and Stan told him that the Jenkintown Acme where he worked was hiring. This was perfect for Paul, as he lived in Jenkintown. Once they began working together their relationship strengthened and they became best friends. While Jenkintown was very convenient for Paul, it wasn't exactly around the corner from Stan's house in Horsham. Perhaps God was at work in bringing Stan to Jenkintown? After all, this is where their relationship began to grow.

Following Stan's crash, Paul visited him every day (yes, every day) while he was in Abington Memorial Hospital. When Stan was moved to Bryn Mawr Rehab, he made the trip twice a week. Perhaps God was at work again? I believe it was Paul's upbringing and his resulting strong character and sense of right and wrong that kept him visiting. He proved to be a truly loyal friend, and his caring extended to Doc and Louise, Stan's brothers, and his extended family. The relationship was and continues to be a source of comfort and joy, which I'll explain below. Perhaps God was at work in this relationship, knowing how important it would be to everyone involved for years to come?

For Doc and Louise, I believe this relationship has filled a massive gap in their life created by Stan's crash and the loss of life's "normal" progression for him. Through us they have been able to experience the milestones of an engagement, a wedding, and "grandchildren." They also enjoy simple pleasures with us, such as pot roast, birthday parties, pool parties, and Disney vacations. Please note that I am not taking anything away from David and Kevin, who have provided all the above and much more.

However, Doc and Louise also had dreams for how Stan's life would unfold. Hopefully, we have lessened the pain of these unfulfilled dreams, provided companionship and joy in the process, and helped with their healing.

As for me and Paul, the relationship we have with Doc and Louise has also filled gaps in our life. We have been unofficially adopted by the Travises and they count our children among their grandchildren. It fills a gap created by the premature deaths of both my mom and Paul's dad, and the traumatic brain injury of my dad. With Doc and Louise we always feel that we have parents by our side, and our kids know the joy of having grandparents.

I am a firm believer that something good always comes out of something bad. In the case of Stan's crash, it has been the beautiful, lasting relationship we have with the Travis family, especially Doc and Louise. I would like to think that it has played a part in their healing. As I said above, perhaps God was at work in this relationship, knowing how important it would be to everyone involved for years to come.

Sincerely,

Linda Cahill

Family Friend and Brain Injury Survivor

My name is Andrew Luke Dooley — Andy. I am a forty-five-year-old male from Horsham, Pennsylvania. Horsham is and was a great place to grow up. I was raised on Maple Avenue a couple of houses up the street from Dr. Stan Travis and his family. Their youngest son, Kevin, is a year younger than me, but back then age didn't make much difference, as all the kids in the neighborhood hung out together playing games — ghost in the graveyard, tag, hide-and-seek — as well as sports. Kevin has two older brothers, Dave and Stan. The kids in the neighborhood often congregated around the Travises' house because it was the center point of many of our houses. Their next-door neighbor had a huge yard we often used for football, whiffle ball, and any other game that needed a field. Oh yeah, the Travises also had a great swimming pool come summertime. Stan, the oldest of the Travis children, was known simply as Stan the Man because he was the eldest, most mature, and biggest guy in the group I hung with. Stan seemed to be a great brother for Kevin and Dave. He needed space, but he could also be protective if called upon.

On July 3, 1985, I was in an auto accident; just me and a telephone pole. Luckily my driver education course in high school had drilled into my head how important it was to wear my seat belt. I was wearing it on that day in July, thank God, and I am still here to talk about it. I spent the rest of July at a local hospital (Abington Memorial Hospital). While still comatose, I was transferred by ambulance to Bryn Mawr Rehabilitation Hospital in Malvern, where I began my lengthy rehabilitation. Still in a coma, there was little to be done, but I slowly regained consciousness and the rehab began. I had therapies six days a week. These included: speech therapy, occupational therapy, physical therapy, and a cognitive retraining program (CRP). I'd see a psychologist once or twice a week as well as a triad of doctors once every couple of weeks for an evaluation. I was released from inpatient therapy in December 1985. I continued outpatient therapy until the following August 1986.

In February 1986, news of Stan's injury reached our household. It was a scary time, but I was confident that Stan was in good hands when I heard he was at Bryn Mawr Rehab. In the summer of '86, I was standing in line at a bank when from out of nowhere I heard this voice call across the bank, "Dooley, it's great to see you, kid." It was Dr. Stan, who wrapped me in one of his signature bear hugs. Dr. Stan was always nice, but I'm not afraid to say he intimidated me a little as a boy. However, at that moment I felt his hug had chased away that fear. That still to this day stands as one of my favorite moments in life.

Yes, I heard about Stan Jr.'s 300 game in bowling, proving he is still the Man...

Andy Dooley

Bowling Industry Manager

My name is William Little, and I am the general manager of Thunderbird Lanes in Warminster, Pennsylvania. I started in the bowling industry when I was thirteen years old and this has basically been what I have done and have known my entire life. I studied psychology for the two and a half years that I went to Kutztown University. I did not complete college because of my passion for bowling and working in the bowling industry. However, some of the things that I did learn while in college were that people are creatures of habit, whether it is in their personal or professional lives, spiritually or non-spiritually. It has been a truth that has driven me to promote and market the industry I work in. I believe that once someone gets hooked on bowling, they continue it as long as they are physically able.

My best day is any day that I see a customer leave my establishment smiling. My worst day is any day that I see a customer leave my establishment not smiling.

When I first met Stan, I knew that he had to have gone through some kind of life-changing experience. My first thoughts were that he had suffered trauma to his head. I have only known Stan for a short period of time. The only experience I have had with Stan or his family has been through the bowling center that Stan bowls at and where he was able to accomplish something special. Stan bowled a perfect 300 game, which for most competitive bowlers is the ultimate goal. I bowled my first 300 game when I was nineteen years old and I remember the feeling I had that night. Now, nineteen years later, I have accomplished that feat forty-one times. When I bowled my fortieth 300 game, the emotion was overwhelming, more so than any of the thirty-nine previous 300 games I had bowled. It took me nineteen years to understand what it felt like again to accomplish something so special, and for me to understand why the accomplishment is so important to the people that achieve it. I was not here the night that Stan bowled his perfect 300 game. I found out the next morning when I came to work. I had known Stan for a short while before he accomplished this, and I knew of his condition and how it had occurred through his crash.

I at first did not believe the person telling me what he had done and I had to look at the scores myself. After thinking about it, it never occurred to me that Stan loved bowling that much. Stan was the perfect example of what I had studied in college for the brief period I was there. He is a creature of habit. And, like all creatures of habit, Stan had worked long enough at something that he loved to perfect it. Regardless of what his physical or mental conditions are, Stan put himself into a place where he was able to do what he knew. He may not know or be able to do things that people without his kind of condition can do, but he is able to bowl, and Stan and his family, perhaps unconsciously, knew that bowling was something Stan was going to be able to do and be good at. For Stan, bowling a 300 game would have been his lifelong dream regardless of his accident. The fact that he went through what he did and he still accomplished it makes it even more special. We should all learn something from Stan. He engulfed himself in something that he is good at and that he enjoys doing. Even if he was great just for that one night, he would still be good. Whether he realizes that or not, I do not know, but I think the people around him do.

William Little

Sister and Godmother

I'm Louise's sister and Stan Jr.'s godmother.

Shortly before Stan's accident I had been laid off from my job. The company had lost a government contract and the entire department had been eliminated. I had worked there for eight years, and was getting better jobs within the company almost every two years. I was devastated and crying. Nothing else opened up within the company and I signed up for unemployment while I looked for another job. At that point I did not realize that our Father had more important things for me to do with my days.

We got a call in the middle of the night about Stan's accident and went to the hospital. He was better when we first saw him, but his condition deteriorated. After that, because I had lost my job, I was able to spend *every day* at the hospital with Louise. At first, Louise and Stan (Doc) never left the hospital, but eventually Doc had to return to work. By the grace of God, because my job had been eliminated, I could go to the hospital every day to be with Louise.

I kept the journal because all the facts and changes in his condition started to blur and I was losing track. The journal was also therapy during all those long and painful hours, days, weeks, and months. I gave Louise the journal when she told me about your interest, so I don't remember when I started keeping track and when I stopped. I had never shown it to anyone before that, although Doc had asked to see it. I just didn't remember what I wrote, or if I wanted to share it. I never went back and reread it.

Some events stand out in my mind, and I am not sure if I even recorded them because I was not sitting in a hall or waiting room at the time. Doc told us that Stan's brain was swelling and it would be necessary to take him to the OR to remove a piece of his brain. That was incomprehensible to me. When they wheeled him out of intensive care to take him to the OR, his head was swollen huge, his tongue was swollen and hanging out of his mouth, his one eye was bandaged, he was black and blue and swollen every-where—he looked like a monster. Some of his friends and his fiancée were with us, and everyone gasped when they saw him. I felt so bad that his friends saw him that way. He was so hand-some before this. We waited until the surgery was done (it was very late); he had survived, and Emil and I went home. We didn't even have time to get to bed before Doc called again and told us that they were taking him back to the OR because his brain was continuing to swell and it was necessary to remove another piece of it. When I hung up the phone, Emil asked me what the call was about. I told him that we had to go back to the hospital; Doc had said that they were taking him back to the OR. Emil asked what for. I told him that I was not sure, because I thought Stan said they were taking another piece of his brain, but I thought I must have misunderstood. They couldn't keep taking pieces of his brain, could they?

I thought maybe I had misunderstood because I couldn't believe it. When we got to the hospital, we found that I had understood correctly.

I walked down the hall with Doc. He was beside himself and desperate. He asked me to pray along with him that our Lord would spare his son and let him live. He said, "I don't even care if he is a vegetable, we can just see him and look at him and be with him." I told him I had been praying and would continue to pray for a complete healing.

Stan was in a medically induced coma for ages. I read magazine articles on boxing to him because I knew he liked the sport. We were told to talk to him, read to him, and so on. When the priest came, I could tell he did not know what to say or do. Louise was the one who took the initiative to lead everyone in reciting the rosary. She kept the scapular on him and any religious relic that was offered to her. We all prayed like crazy, silently or together aloud.

Louise always thought positive thoughts or was unrealistic; I wasn't sure which it was. I was with her one day when she was talking to, I think it was the neuro or orthopedic surgeon, and she asked if Stan would be able to water-ski again, since he loved it so much and was so good at it. The surgeon looked at her in amazement and shock, not sure if even then she realized the gravity of the situation, or if she just believed in miracles. I don't think he even responded.

There was one thing that angered and irritated me in the hospital. Dr. Pagnanelli would come to give an update of Stan's condition and would take Doc down the hall and speak to him. I would feel so angry at his passing right by Louise. Who did he think she was? Did she look like a lady sitting in the hall outside intensive care waiting for a bus? All the other doctors would include her in the updates. It was her son, too, not just Doc's.

My son was getting married in May and I did not want to take the time away from the hospital to shop for a dress for the wedding. It all seemed so inconsequential when we were dealing with life issues. Nothing I tried on pleased me, or made me feel happy. I felt too sad to feel pleased with a dress. Louise and Doc came to the wedding, and it was the first day Louise had left Stan's side since the crash.

His closest friends and fiancée continued to visit in the hospital from February to May, and then at Bryn Mawr Rehab. The other momentous occasion occurred at Bryn Mawr. He had not been able to say a word since his brain surgery, not a "Hi," not a "Mom," nothing. One night his friends were playing the radio outside where they had wheeled him. The song came on the radio and he started to smile and sing along, "Do wah diddy diddy dum diddy do." We were all shocked and elated to hear his first words.

Louise tends to think positive regarding her son. She is a wonderful mother and caregiver, and I feel certain that he has come so far because of her. I know she gains her strength from God and her prayer group. Their life is kind of like BC and AD.

Thank you for giving voice to Stan's experiences and the miracle of his life.

With appreciation,

Helen

Clinical Case Coordinator and Certified Brain Injury Specialist

I was exposed to this industry at a very early age. My older sister, who is like a second mother to me, started Main Line Rehabilitation Associates in 1986, when I was twelve years old. She used to tutor me when I was in high school and it would take place at the original MLRA office. I was exposed to individuals with traumatic brain injuries and it left a lasting impression on me. When I was around sixteen years old, a client of MLRA came and spoke to my high school soccer team about drinking and driving. The client was a great high school athlete, but was involved in a car accident when he was drinking and driving, leaving him partially paralyzed with a TBI. At that point, I knew I was going to be in this profession. When I went to college, I majored in psychology and did my internships through MLRA. After graduating from college and working for MLRA for the summer, I decided that I was not cut out for this line of work and changed professions for approximately five years. After losing my job due to cutbacks as a result of 9/11, my sister approached me with an opportunity to come back to work for MLRA on a temporary basis until I decided what I wanted to do. I started with one client, and provided services for him twelve hours a week. Eventually, I was given another client, and within six months, I was a full-time employee. I am not sure what changed inside me after five years of being out of this profession, but when I returned it felt right. For seven years, I provided one-on-one therapy for individuals with TBI and other neurological disorders. Three years ago, I became a clinical coordinator and now manage approximately twenty cases. I also am involved in the marketing of our company.

I believe I work in a great profession. Our clinical staff goes out every day and works with individuals in their natural environments, and truly makes a positive difference in their lives. We assist these individuals with daily activities that would be impossible to complete independently. Most of the people we work with have limited supports, and struggle with memory, problem solving, initiation, scheduling/planning, communication, social behavior, and cognition. Our staff assists in the development of strategies that help those individuals make it through a typical day. From all the feedback we receive from our consumers, our services are vital for keeping them out of nursing homes or assisted living environments.

Unfortunately, due to many budget cuts at the Department of Welfare in the state of Pennsylvania, it is becoming harder and more challenging to continue providing services. The state is making it harder to apply for services, harder to receive services, and harder for companies like MLRA to provide services. As an organization, we are always scrambling to meet the new requirements so we can continue to work with our individuals.

In my profession, you learn to cherish the good days when progress is made. The nature of brain injury is that progress is

152

slow, and at times you may not make progress for long periods of time. It is also the nature of the business to deal with constant barriers due to difficult family members, cognitive deficit areas, financial constraints, and other issues. More often than not, our staff is reacting to negative occurrences, so when something positive happens, you take a lot of pride in being a part of it. For me, my best day occurred when I assisted one of my clients with moving into a new apartment. This individual's wife had left him after he had a brain aneurism, and he had moved into a horrific living situation. It was in one of the worst parts of the city, and he had moved in with a woman who stole money from him on a daily basis. He was being exploited and taken advantage of, and his team knew that he needed to be removed from this situation. Unfortunately, he did not have the tools to recognize that he was being taken advantage of, and was unable to leave on his own. With the assistance of the whole team, we were able to make him aware of the situation and assisted him with locating a new apartment. This was the first time that he was on his own after his injury, and I truly believe that getting him out of that situation saved his life. He is now remarried and living a productive life.

The worst day I have experienced during my time at MLRA occurred a little less than a year ago. It was the day I found out that one of my clients, that I had worked with in different capacities over the course of seven years, was killed outside his home. I worked with this man in his home for five years and then coordinated his case when I became a case coordinator. It is natural to become close with a client after this much time, and I also developed a great relationship with his ailing mother. My client was in a wheelchair and had very poor eyesight as a result of multiple brain tumors he had at an early age. He would go out into his community independently all the time, but there were occasions when he had falls or got stuck and needed assistance. At the time of his death, he was approximately fifty years old. One night he went outside to a walkway behind his apartment complex and got caught on a set of train tracks, and was killed when he was hit by a train. Although at the time of the accident,

I was not working with this client anymore, it was devastating news to hear. I represented my company at the service, and when I spoke to his mother, she was incredibly grateful for all the work we had done with her son. She was also convinced that her son was in a better place and not suffering anymore. I had one client that I work with pass away when I first started at MLRA, and this situation was very difficult to deal with. In this business, you learn to understand that our client's health may deteriorate and some may even die.

I have been working in this field for approximately ten years now and still enjoy it immensely. Nothing is more satisfying than knowing that you have made a positive contribution to someone's life. There are moments when you appreciate that you have been directly responsible for making someone's life more fulfilling. It is a very difficult field to work in, and I believe it takes a special person to do this type of work. There are so many barriers that must be overcome, such as limited support, deficits from the injury, financial constraints, funding issues, and resistance from those that you are trying to help. It can also be difficult to work with individuals that do not have the awareness that they need the help. Frustrations may arise because progress can be slow, and making improvements in some lives may not be visible for long periods of time. However, there is nothing more gratifying than when a client says to you, "Thank you so much for your help, I don't know what I would do without you."

God? I am Roman Catholic and believe in God and believe in faith.

Stan has significant impairments and deficits as a result of the head trauma and frontal lobe issues.

> **Aphasia**: The inability to break down a task into steps. For example, we know that if we want to clean a room we would get the necessary cleaning supplies, clean the room, and then put the cleaning supplies away. Someone with aphasia doesn't understand these steps are involved, but with a visual aid or diagram they can carry out the task. People with deficit also have difficulty formulating

sentences. They know what they want to say but have difficulty getting it out.

Motor Apraxia: Losing the ability to carry out certain movements. For example, there may be balance issues and results in multiple falls when bowling.

It's interesting to note that we have charted our scores when bowling together. The first time we played he beat me. I have bowled and am okay, but after he got warmed up, Stan absolutely destroyed me!

Planning and Scheduling: They need help maintaining. For example, Stan takes about twenty-four various pills a day. We help him load his pill case so that he takes them correctly.

Cognitive Issues:
Almost zero short-term memory
Initiation/motivation issues
Fatigues easily
Severe seizure history
Problem solving: Prompting and cueing - the ability to come up with solutions. For example, if I have an ache, I may rest, take an aspirin, stretch, monitor the pain, see a doctor. In Stan's case, he would just live with it.

Attention deficit
Visual perception

I first met Stan around 1990. Right off the bat he struck me as being low-key, friendly, cool, calm, and collected. Some clients are very resistant. He completes chores, is involved in sports activities, and has a job at Acme. Prior to the accident Stan was very active. He seems to be completely happy with his job, bowling, water sports, and family gatherings. His mom, Louise, helps with his treatment plan. Stan is lucky to have a good social support system. I have known him for ten years. He does not dwell on things. Although he may be unhappy at times, he may not have the awareness of knowing what he has lost. Stan has a lot of support. For example, staff goes with him to Acme to help him complete his responsibilities. We are his job coach.

The data has shown that the healing that has happened is usually in the form of a bell curve. After head trauma there is an increase in activity and progress, and then at around fifteen years post injury there is a plateau, after which time health problems begin to occur and aging may happen at a quicker rate.

For Stan, there seem to be no physical limitations; it's surprising he is almost 100 percent physically.

What we know is that when strategies are created and used consistently, the greater the success for the individual. Stan has strategies to help him through his day:

- Visual aids
- Notebooks
- Flashcards
- Checklists
- Charts

For example, at Acme he has a card with the store layout, an aisle listing, and he carries a recorder to remember. At home, he has a checklist before he goes out, a laminated chore card to clean the bathroom and his bedroom, and a memory log of past conversations.

There is a survey that we give. A "How happy are you?" survey. What we see is that depression is normal. What we have seen with Stan Travis is that he is a happy guy and seems to have achieved acceptance a long time ago.

Phone interview with Mark Cola

Main Line Rehabilitation Associates, Inc.

Gastroenterologist

I met Stan's parents when I went into practice as a gastroenterologist at Abington Memorial Hospital. Of course, Stan Senior (Doc), as a community family physician, would refer patients to our practice for GI care. I chose to be a doctor, and specifically this subspecialty of internal medicine, as a result of being the daughter of two physicians. My father was a general surgeon who, together with my mother, a civilian physician working for the army, would have dinner conversations discussing interesting cases they had. It was hearing about gallbladders, diverticulosis, colectomies, and ulcer surgery that made gastrointestinal diseases seem like a good field to pursue, and it came easily to me.

There are many "best days," as I am blessed to have many appreciative patients who tell me they are feeling better or are reassured they do not have a dreaded disease. The worst day is the day I don't give my all to any one patient. I too get frustrated and discouraged with lack of progress or resolution of a problem.

I am not a religious person, but have faith in the human spirit that one can and will gather strength from somewhere deep inside in order to survive. I believe Stan and his family have an incredible ability to draw on that strength.

I see from reviewing Stan's record that I first became involved in his care in 1990, when he was found to have a hepatitis C infection involving his liver. This viral infection was transmitted via the multiple blood transfusions he had received as a result of his car crash. At that time, a relatively new treatment had become available for HCV (hepatitis C virus), Intron A (interferon). Before undergoing treatment a liver biopsy was necessary, which he underwent without incident. The results showed mild inflammation of the triads, an area of the liver that holds the many blood vessels and bile ducts, and there was no sign of liver cell damage or signs of scarring. Because of potential side effects of the drug therapy and the mild nature of the findings, the therapy was not initiated in hopes that newer or more effective, safe therapy would come along in the future.

As time went on, it became apparent that he should initiate treatment, and three weekly self-injections of Intron A were initiated in 1995. He would continue these injections for a full year. He would require close monitoring of his liver test and watching for side effects. He did have minor issues with injection site pain and redness, some aches and flu-like symptoms, as well

157

as variable gut complaints, but for the most part he was able to endure the full treatment, with disappearance of the virus and normalization of the liver enzymes. However, it became apparent that by six months following cessation of the drug, there were particles measurable once again. This was closely followed for a few months. My contact with Stan ended there, and I have no detail whether or not additional treatment was needed.

In 2000, Stan returned to our care under Dr. Jeffrey Berman, who specializes in liver disease. At that time there was no evidence of the HCV in his system. Stan had apparently cleared the virus completely. A wonderful ending!

I'm sad to say that I have not had any direct contact with Stan since 1996. I have only heard snippets of news from his parents from time to time, and of course I read about his wonderful achievement of bowling a perfect game. I hope to see him face-to-face again someday.

Dr. Anne Saris

Orthopedic Surgeon

I remember that I didn't operate on Stan right away because he had a severe head injury. A couple of days later I put a plate on his femur. He had a bad fracture. I remember being so exhausted after that case. The resident who assisted me was a strong football player. I'm glad I had him with me, as it took a lot of strength to work on the femur. I can't say enough about how much physical strength and mental perseverance was needed. It was a few days after the trauma, so it was even more difficult to work on it. From an orthopedic standpoint he did very well.

And, we're not talking a five- or six-hole plate. We are talking twelve holes or so.

I remember Dr. Pagnanelli (I believe that was his name) wheeling Stan back to surgery for a second time. He was pushing the bed, support staff was around him, oxygen was going, and they were moving fast—running him up there.

I recall Dr. Pagnanelli saying something like, "We gave him everything we can...he's gonna go...he's on the verge...I gotta take some more brain tissue." They opened him up and took out more of his brain. This was a tough case. We didn't think he would come around. I am surprised he's doing what he's doing.

I've been retired for sixteen years, and I sometimes look back at some of what I did. I can't believe that we do what we do as orthopedic surgeons. We just threw ourselves into our work. We did what needed to be done.

We do know that the brain in a young person can regenerate dramatically. For example, I recall a patient being unconscious for six to eight months. He was strapped to the bed and had to be turned every twelve hours or so. One day he wakes up. There are people in the room playing chess. First thing he says is something like, "Move the white king." And, these are people who didn't have a head injury! In Stan's case, him doing what he is doing is even more remarkable.

Phone interview with Dr. Paul Sweterlitsch

Behavioral Neurologist

My name is Dr. David Long. I am a neurologist and behavioral neurologist, cognitive and relationship. I am also the medical director of the Brain Injury Unit at Bryn Mawr Rehabilitation Hospital.

Intellectually, I was drawn to this field. I was an orderly at a young age in a nursing home during one summer. While I was at college my stepfather had a stroke. I wanted med school, but didn't know what aspect. I was exposed to so many people along the way—fantastic people. I was at Hahnemann and Chester Crozier Medical Center, and they said you gotta go to Boston to the Aphasia Center. This is where I was exposed to trauma. I've been doing this ever since. I'm a bit unusual in this sense.

My best days practicing are when someone has a significant breakthrough and we are not sure why, but they turn it around. It's also gratifying when we make a therapeutic move and it works. The worst day is when we thought they were doing okay but then they go sour.

We treat people who have had brain injuries. Some have profound injuries and recover, while others may be less severe in many ways, but don't seem to reintegrate into society and the family.

When we first saw Stan, he was emerging from the coma; starting over. He was in amazingly bad shape; very severe. He had a lot of hemorrhaging, significant visual impairment, frontal lobe injuries, and language problems. He had seizure problems early on and Dr. Sperling was called in, and the seizures are in check now. He was (and is) weaker on the right side of the body, and has unusual behaviors sometimes because of the connecting fibers between the right and left side of the brain. The fact that he has been doing very basic, everyday activities is incredible. The fact that he is doing many things above and beyond everyday basic living is wild!

Stan Travis is a message of hope, a living testimony. This is a wonderful thing for people to see. The brain has the ability to recover. Back in the day, we didn't understand the plasticity of the brain and that what we do determines how the brain functions. For example, we know today that brain cells that do activity A can take on activity B, and can then take on activity C, and so on.

What may be very important to note is the positive approach that Stan and his family have displayed despite all their obstacles. There is no question that motivation and having a positive attitude can be the biggest difference — it's just huge. This seems to be the natural way that the Travises think. They are the nicest people you can imagine. To see Stan overcome such adversity and bowl a 300 game is a story of inspiration and hope. The Travises are loved.

Phone interview with Dr. David Long

Neurosurgeon

I recall the day that Stan herniated in ICU. I had tried every nonsurgical means available, but he continued to deteriorate. His father was with me every step of the way. Stan had deteriorated rather abruptly, so I ordered a stat CT scan of his head. Dr. Travis and I went to see Stan's latest CT scan together. As we looked at the images we both knew the situation. Stan had a large blood clot and a great deal of swelling that was compressing his brain. He was dying.

Much of his brain had been pushed to the other side of the head, and it also was pushed down toward his brain stem. His pupils were dilated and time was of the essence. It was a difficult position for me. I had known Dr. T for several years and had had many patients in common with him, and he was a friend. But this was personal and very emotionally charged. I found it extremely difficult to tell him that I had to operate to remove the blood clot and damaged brain tissue from his son. Dr. T was clearly in shock, but told me to do what I had to do. We took Stan directly to the operating room. I quickly opened and removed the clot as well as injured brain. This gave his normal brain room and relieved the pressure.

I'm not certain, but I think the injury was mostly to Stan's left temporal lobe. He came back to us after surgery. However, he had severe brain damage and was not able to talk. Very slowly the swelling decreased, and he eventually recovered enough to go to a rehabilitation facility. As the months passed I got regular updates from Dr. T and Louise. Dr. T gave me a photo of Stan water-skiing. I still have that on the wall next to my desk, to remind me that working hard for a patient, in what seems like a hopeless situation, can give good results. Stan Sr. and Louise were amazing throughout this ordeal. They never lost hope. They didn't care how he turned out. They just wanted their son alive.

Sincerely,

Dr. David M. Pagnanelli

Father and Doctor

Through all these years of Stan's injury, I have worn two hats: father and doctor. This at times was extremely difficult, especially through the early months. Thinking as a father who may lose his son, thinking as a doctor who may not be able to prevent his death.

I was the last to see him on February 27, 1986, when he kissed me good-bye on his way to enjoy an evening with friends. The next time he came home, except for weekends, was November 6, 1986. It's hard to write 1986 — so long ago.

His early hospital days were the worst, especially after March 5, 1986, when his brain swelled and the beginning of his life-and-death struggle began. As a father praying to God for his survival; as a doctor looking at CT scans, lab studies, and X-rays, which all showed the massive injuries to his head and body. Father and doctor thought of if he survived, how would he live his life? If he died, thought of organ donation.

Through all those early months and to today we have had tremendous support from family and friends. I cried alone, we cried together; I prayed alone, we prayed together. I worked in my office, getting out early to go to the hospital, always waiting for a call from Louise to give me updates. Difficult times — again, father/doctor.

The years passed, some very slowly, some more quickly. Stan not only survived but began a new life; different than it would have been, but much better than it could have been. God gave Stan his life back to enjoy to his ability, and it is not a bad life.

He has never struggled with anger. He has never suffered with depression. He has great love for his family and friends. He continues to have physical and mental challenges. He has overcome some; some will remain forever. His life enjoyments are simple: playing cards and checkers, watching TV, the Phillies, the Miami Dolphins, and especially his family, friends, and bowling — his passion. Every achievement both physical and mental is major because each is difficult. As you know, his physical achievement which changed his life and began great healing for his brothers and friends was on January 25, 2011, when he bowled a perfect 300 game. Absolutely never expected; absolutely incredible! It made him famous; it made us all proud.

When his journey will end, we don't know. We do know we have been blessed. Many prayers have been answered, miracles have happened, and there are more prayers for his future to be answered. We know that with God, with prayer, and with his wonderful family and friends, Stan will enjoy the rest of his life, until he meets with his Lord and thanks him in person. I am sure he will find a bowling alley in heaven.

Love,

Dad

CLOSING THOUGHTS

FAITH

A recovery from anything, I thought, is a process that is ongoing. We've been told there is no 100 percent. I choose not to think about that. Our journey isn't over. Currently, Stan is having some neurological difficulty. He is having some problems with his steps and approach when bowling and getting his hand to release the ball. This causes him to fall sometimes. I've called his neurologist, checked his defect to make sure his brain shunt is working, and we've tried different things ourselves. Perhaps we'll contact a physical therapist to see what he suggests. After all, Stan had lost his entire right side when he went into the coma and he rehabbed it back. We did it before, and this time it doesn't compare.

I can remember when he came out of the coma and I was giving him a pep talk. Not knowing at the time he probably didn't know who I was or understand what I was saying.

It's like at the hospital when people would ask me what his prognosis was. I replied that I didn't know, that I hadn't asked the doctors. What I saw on these people's faces was a patronizing, sympathetic smile. My thoughts were that if I ask and they say he'll never do something, I may not try. Not knowing, we went for it all. I felt the more we tried for, the more we'd get. IT WORKED! I wouldn't take "negative anything" into my mind and my heart.

We stared into each other's eyes. I promised him I'd be with him every step of the way, but he couldn't give up. We haven't and we won't!

That goes for you, too. Keep the faith and never give up!

In spite of having difficulty getting his body to do what his brain is telling it to do and having trouble bowling, which is his favorite thing to do in life, Stan woke up one morning in early May 2012 and the first thing out of his mouth was, "I'm lucky, Mom."

"Yes," I responded, "you are blessed, but what are you referring to?"

He said, "I'm not mad, or sad, or mean...I'm blessed."

When will the Lord complete the healing he has begun in Stan? Who knows. What will the future hold? God only knows. What I do know is that he will continue to walk beside us all the way. What'll happen to Stan when his dad and I are gone? I have to place my son in his hands and trust.

Louise

We are either connected or disconnected. We are either plugged in or unplugged. When we are feeling good, happy, and harmonious—truly—we are in touch with God. Everything just seems to happen and to flow. When we are tuned in, we are motivated to do our work. We either progress or regress. There is no standing still. What we focus on happens and what we don't give our attention to disappears. Take some time to think about this.

There is love all around us. *It* holds us in the palm of *Its* hand, gently stroking us, nurturing us, cheering us on. The love is in our very being, and when we are in touch with *It*, *It* shows in our actions, our smile, and our words. *It*'s beautiful. *It*'s wonderful. *It*'s your life. What are you going to do with *It*?

Bill

Stan, Louise, and Doc are available
to share their inspirational, motivational, and educational story
with your community, organization, school, and company.

Contact Bill at:
Bill@Fipsila.com

The Journey
Stan's Story
From Death to Perfection
is available directly from the publisher at:
www.createspace.com/4030664

A discount code is available on Fipsila.com
Bill and Louise donate

10% of their royalty.

Who's Louise?

Louise was born in Nicetown, Pennsylvania (PA). She attended Philadelphia Public Schools and graduated from the Abington School District while living in Roslyn, PA. Aspiring to be a florist, she took Distributive Education courses in high school and worked in a flower shop as part of the program. Louise was president of the Future Business Leaders of America at her school. During the summer of 1957, she met Stan Travis (Doc) a pre-med student at LaSalle College in Philadelphia. They fell in love. To save money for their wedding in June 1962, Louise sacrificed her career as a florist and took a job as a sales rep with Bell Telephone. Doc was studying at Philadelphia College of Osteopathic Medicine (P.C.O.M.).

In November 1963, Stan Travis III was born. After Doc graduated from P.C.O.M. they moved to Michigan for his internship where their second son David was born in December 1964. They moved to Horsham, PA in 1967 where Doc opened his family practice. Their third son Kevin arrived in August 1968. Doc continues to serve Horsham and the surrounding communities today.

The Horsham area was and continues to be a very close community of people and families. Louise is still very much involved in this community: family, home, church, and of course gardening!

Who's Bill?

Ms. Jenkins. Late 1960s. Kindergarten. I remember like yesterday listening to her stories. She asked us to make stuff like animals, objects, and people. One time I made a fish. We told stories about what we made. I don't remember the exact stories but I do remember being a little kid who was fascinated about all of this. Stories about people, places, and things would continue to fascinate me. Always. Everywhere. It's laughable!

At school, at home, and at work I would be called the guy who loved people, travel, and exploration. I always had a story and always encouraged others to tell theirs. What I found was that no matter where I went, who I spoke with and listened to, and what I observed the point was that there is a common element in every person, every animal, every thing, and every where. What is *it*?

It is life. Life. Growth. Change. Life is awesome. Life is good. Life is *it*. I became inspired to write about *it*, about life. Fipsila became the vehicle. People. Animals. Nature.

The Fipsila story is at Fipsila.com. There are books for children, teenagers, young adults, and adults – native English speakers and those who speak English as a second language. Fipsila books, games, and services are all about the common thread that link us to each other. In every culture and in every person there is life.

What's your story?

Who's Bill? Tough to define, right? Here's the nickel tour ... Bill has been an educator, coach, and public speaker in different settings in Belize, Guatemala, Peru, France, and the USA. He has taught and spoken in the public and private sectors. He has facilitated the learning process with people age eight to age seventy-six, including Guatemalan children and adults in Corporate America and France.

171

Bill is an author. He's grateful. He looks around and says: "Is this amazing or what?." He has had many influential role models over the years.

Bill is an accomplished triathlete: one hundred triathlons, eight Ironmans. He has a personal best of 1:00.29 at the Sprint distance and 10:34.46 at the Ironman distance.

Bill has lived on three continents. He enjoys family, friends, and being fit at his farms, one in the foothills of the Pyrenees in France, and the other at Ruger Ridge near Prescott, Arizona, in the USA. He helps French Airbus employees understand every-day American Anglo Saxon English.

Bill's first book -
Fipsila®, My Story
An interactive book for children and their parents to create and
share their story
Read. Write. Draw. Color. Share.
Available soon directly from the publisher at:
www.createspace.com/4136297

Bill's second book -
The Adventures of Fipsila® USA – France
fourteen short stories
Available directly from the publisher at:
www.creatspace.com/3963782
Note: One of these short stories tells about how Bill and the
Travises became connected:
Fipsila Watches A Perfect Game – Stan Travis Bowls 300

Discounts are available at
Fipsila.com

Bill's series of books:
Bill's next book is, *Twenty*, one man's journey to trust, feel, and
love.
William has travelled the world. He found love during his trek.
He thinks.
Instead, he found that he has a complete inability to trust ... any-
one, especially a woman.
Perhaps this time will be different. Maybe!
Coming soon
Fipsila.com

Made in the USA
Charleston, SC
03 March 2013